66 Projects, Activities, and Crafts for Children

Hands-on FAITH

**The Rosary • Morning Prayer • Liturgy of the Word
Liturgy of the Eucharist • Vessels and Vestments
The Evangelists • Noah's Ark • Jonah and the Whale
Wedding at Cana • Angels • Advent Calendar • Christmas
Easter • St. Patrick's Shamrock • Legend of St. Valentine
Blessing of Pets • and many, many more**

Mary Doerfler Dall

ave maria press   Notre Dame, IN

This book is dedicated to
Susan Gilchrist
and to my husband, Dan,
and to our children,
Erin, Amanda and Mike.
A special thanks also to Mike Amodei,
my editor, for his encouragement, help, and support.

Contents

Chapter 5: Holy Days and Church Seasons 89

Chapter 6: More Faith Sharing 107

Endnotes 127

Introduction

Children learn best by doing. There is hardly a parent, catechist, teacher, coach, drama instructor, or any other person who works with kids who would dispute that!

Hands-on Faith was created to answer the need for more hands-on lessons in the area of religious education. This book includes over sixty-five projects, activities, and crafts that will help children learn the key elements of their faith by actually doing the majority of the hands-on lessons themselves.

The projects, activities, and crafts here are meant to supplement religious education efforts already in place. *Hands-on Faith* is divided into six chapters to help organize the material by theme, but each lesson, activity, or craft is self-contained and can be used in conjunction with a variety of units in your religion curriculum. The chapter themes are as follows:

- *Prayer.* The lessons are designed to encourage both personal and communal prayer.

- *Liturgy.* The church's public prayer is best expressed in the sacrament of Eucharist. This chapter looks at both the liturgy of the word and the liturgy of eucharist.

- *The Bible.* Scripture stories are a foundation of our faith. Activities and crafts allow for expression and retention of their dramatic lessons.

- *Legends and Lore.* The church is resplendent with legends and lore that have developed as part of our tradition. This chapter uses many natural symbols to teach important truths.

- *Holy Days and Church Seasons.* The church year offers opportunities to decorate classrooms and homes with elements of the holidays and seasons like Advent, Lent, and Easter.

- *More Faith Sharing.* The final chapter is a collection of several other crafts and activities, including one for a blessing of pets and another thanking God for the gift of nature.

Remember that the purpose of the chapters is to help you more easily locate an activity or craft that might fit your lesson theme. Many of the individual activities could easily fit under more than one chapter heading.

Notes for Doing the Activities and Crafts

All the activities and crafts in *Hands-on Faith* can be easily completed in a short amount of time by most elementary-age children. Little instruction besides the simple directions included with each activity and craft is needed.

These projects require a minimum of supplies. Usually common supplies like glue, scissors, and crayons are all that is needed. When additional supplies are called for, they normally consist of things like empty egg cartons, toothpicks, drinking straws, craft sticks, and the like. A list of special materials needed is included with each activity or craft.

Moreover, a short introduction and complete directions provide ample background for an adult to both explain the purpose of the activity or craft and its connection with our faith.

Many of the activities and crafts in *Hands-on Faith* are designed for easy reproduction and for use in a parish or school religious education program. However, the book can also be used in an individualized setting in which the pages are removed from the book and the activity is completed without interfering with the integrity of the remaining pages. This feature makes *Hands-on Faith* ideal for children to do both as part of family projects and as other home schooling lessons.

1
Prayer

Prayer is an important part of our lives.

We need prayer. Prayer is our connection to God.

It is our way of talking, sharing, and expressing our deepest feelings, our deepest thoughts and desires to God.

Prayer forges our relationship with the Almighty.

The activities in this chapter are designed to encourage prayer as we establish the important place that prayer has in our lives.

Heritage Prayers

We are a diverse nation of backgrounds, languages, and cultures. We share prayers that have been handed down from generations past—sometimes in different languages. Prayers taught to us in childhood have a special place in our hearts.

When I was growing up my parents often spoke in German—especially when they didn't want us to know what they were talking about! To this day, my brothers and sisters and I will often answer "*danke*" for "thank you" and "*bitte*" for "you're welcome" in common conversation. Perhaps the most important German taught to me by my parents was a little prayer that I too have passed on to my own children. Now, our grandson also recites this prayer.

Here is my German heritage prayer:

German:

Ich bin klein.
Mein Herz ist rein.
Soll niemand drin wohnen.
Als Jesus allein.
Author Unknown

English:

I am small.
My heart is pure.
No one should live there.
But Jesus, alone.

Activities:

- Have the children ask their parents and grandparents to share a "heritage prayer" with them. Tell them to print the prayer and bring it to class to share. Another option is to have the students look up prayers in other languages in reference books or on the Internet.

- Display a large world map and talk about how God's love is everywhere in the world. Place the children's printed prayers around the edges of the map. Connect the prayer to its nation of origin with a piece of bright, colored yarn.

- You may wish to turn this map and prayer display into a permanent bulletin board, allowing children to bring in prayers throughout the year.

A Prayer Table for Young Children

Provide space for a prayer table as pictured below. Place a bible, flowers, candle, and cloth on the table. Create a border around the table using the children's names on the patterns below. (Directions and additional activity suggestions on page 12.)

A Prayer Table for Young Children

Directions:

1. Cut out and color a doll for your gender.
2. Print your name on the doll's t-shirt or dress. Or, glue a photo of yourself to the doll.
3. Hole punch dolls at hands and string on a piece of yarn. String yarn together with the other children's dolls and drape around the table.

Additional Activities:

*   Allow each child a turn holding a crucifix while a scripture passage is read aloud. Choose another child to hold the bible while the teacher reads the passage.
*   An individual paper doll representing each child, that the child has colored and decorated, may be placed on a stand as the child has a turn helping at the table. (See the drawing above.)

The Rosary

The rosary is a special devotion to the Blessed Mother. Children love the tactile sensation of touching a rosary. They should be instructed to say the prayers of the rosary while reflecting on the beautiful mysteries that are assigned to specific beads. A brief overview of the rosary and a visual craft will help children see how the prayers of the rosary form a circle of love and help us reflect on the mysteries.

The Mysteries:

Glorious Mysteries

1. The Resurrection

2. The Ascension

3. The Descent of the Holy Spirit

4. The Assumption

5. The Coronation

Joyous Mysteries

1. The Annunciation

2. The Visitation

3. The Nativity

4. The Presentation

5. Finding of Jesus in the Temple

The Sorrowful Mysteries

1. The Agony in the Garden

2. The Scourging at the Pillar

3. The Crowning With Thorns

4. The Carrying of the Cross

5. The Crucifixion

The Rosary

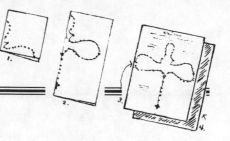

Special Materials Needed:
- single hole punch

Directions:
1. This page must follow a very specific fold. First, fold the page on the dotted horizontal center line. Then, fold again on vertical center line. The x's will show (fig. 1).
2. Using a single hole-punch, punch out the x's *only*.
3. Open. Fold the page again on the vertical center line only. Hole punch the *'s and half punch the •'s (fig. 2).
4. Open the page. Draw in the *chain* lines (fig. 3).
5. Place a sheet of colored construction paper under the page so that the colored paper shows through making colored beads. Glue the edges of the page to the colored sheet of paper (fig. 4).

Additional Activity:

Use colored hole punch dots to make a rosary on a white sheet of paper. Instruct the children to start at the cross and work the circle from both ends. Have them glue in place if desired. Pencil in the lines of the chain.

Thank You 'Copters

We pray for a lot of reasons. We pray to ask God for favors, to praise God's goodness and to offer God our thanks.

God rains down many good things on us. Our prayers of thanksgiving are joyous prayers. We celebrate God's goodness with a happy heart.

These little 'copters hold special thank you notes. After they are completed, take them out to a courtyard area and watch them "rain down" our *thank yous*.

Special Materials Needed:
- paper clips

Directions:
1. Cut out the 'copter on the outside dark lines.
2. Carefully cut the center line.
3. Fold on the dotted lines.
4. Write something you are thankful for on the "thank you" line.
5. Color or decorate the 'copter as you wish.
6. Fold flap A inside.
7. Fold the other flap over flap A.
8. Place a paperclip at the bottom as a weight (fig. 1).
9. Take the 'copter outside or into a large room. Fold the top pieces down (fig. 2) and toss the 'copter high. It will fall down and spin around.
10. As you toss or catch the 'copters repeat your thank you prayers.

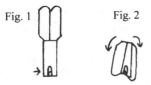

Fig. 1   Fig. 2

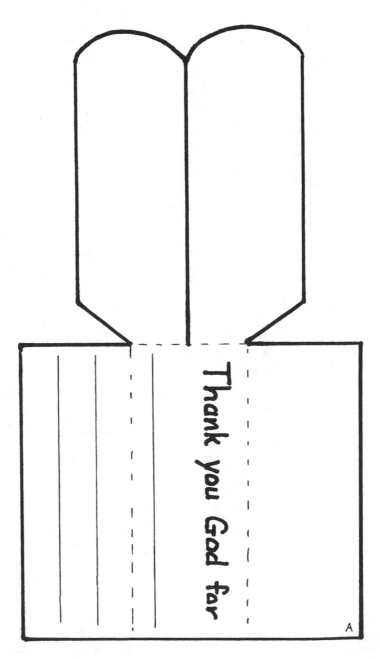

Thank you God for

A

Thank You 'Copters

God rains down blessings on us. We thank God for all our blessings.

Color and decorate this page. (If this page is used as a separate activity draw 'copters and other children in the blank space.)

God's Love Grows and Grows

God's love is not finite; it is infinite. God's love grows and grows. God's love will always find you and be there for you. You can always count on God.

A heart symbol is often used to express love. This heart reminds us how God's love continually grows, reaching out to us.

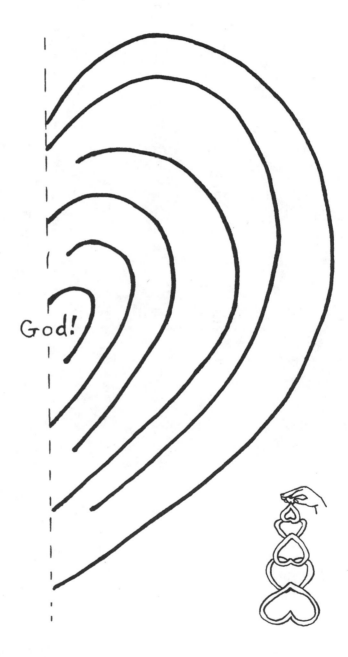

Directions:
1. Fold on the vertical dotted line.
2. Hold the fold and carefully cut *exactly* along the dark lines.
3. Open the page.
4. Hold the small inner heart and allow the outer hearts to fan out.

God's Love Grows and Grows

fig. 1

fig. 2

fig. 3

Additional Activities:

*   Precut hearts of all sizes and allow the children to glue them randomly on the cut-out heart from the previous page (fig. 1).
*   Write "God's Love" in the center of a sheet of large posterboard. Have the students glue hearts in random places on the center and edge (fig. 2).
*   Younger children may have trouble completing the activity on page 17. Instead, cut the hearts separately and have them link the cut hearts to form a mobile.

Let Go of Anger

As the scriptures say, "Do not let the sun go down on your anger" (Eph 4:26). When we are angry, we can have clouded thinking. Anger can make us only see our problem or disappointment. It often closes our eyes and ears to finding a solution.

Prayer can have a very calming affect. You might hear someone say to "count to ten" before you allow yourself to say or do anything when you're angry. Prayer is like a "counting to ten" with a purpose. When you stop to pray about your anger, you put your need for calm into words. Also, you realize that you have a friend in God and that you are no longer alone with your anger.

Dialogue with the children about things that make them angry. Also, remind them that it is helpful to talk with God before making any decisions based in anger. Tell them they can repeat the short mantra, "Come, Lord Jesus" when feelings of anger overwhelm them.

Directions:
1. Cut the rectangle on the dark lines.
2. Fold on the dotted line.
3. On one side draw a picture of yourself praying.
4. On the other side, write "Come, Lord Jesus" or another prayer you call on when angry.

(See page 20 for a separate activity)

Let Go of Anger

In the left column, write several things that make you angry. In the right column, write a possible solution for each thing that makes you angry or words of Jesus that can help you handle your anger.

What Makes Me Angry   **What I Can Do About It**

_____   _____

_____   _____

_____   _____

_____   _____

The Gift of Night and Day

This activity can help the child visualize day and night as the balance of *busy* (moving clouds) and *calm* (stars).

Note: This activity can be made in a larger size and used as a single visual by the catechist.

(Directions follow on page 22.)

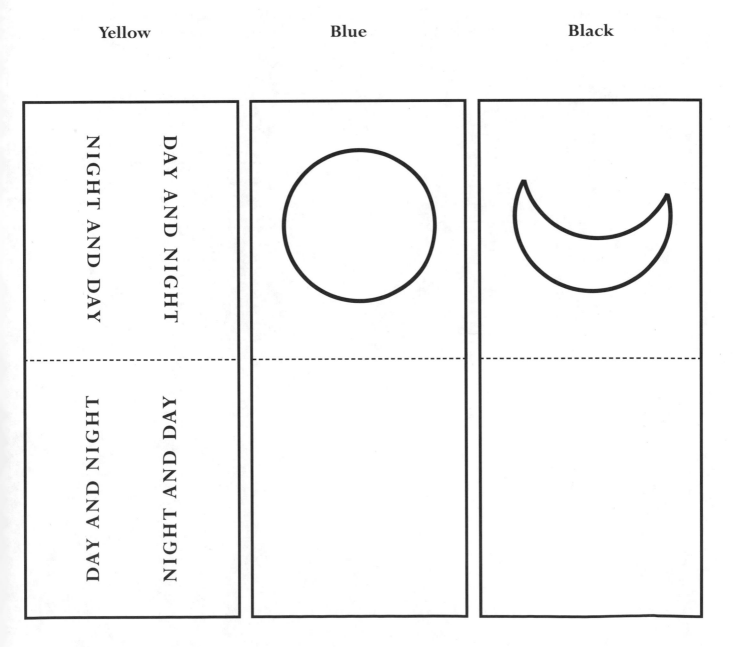

Yellow   Blue   Black

NIGHT AND DAY   DAY AND NIGHT

DAY AND NIGHT   NIGHT AND DAY

The Gift of Night and Day

Special Materials Needed:
- blue, black, and yellow crayons
- cotton balls
- sticker stars

Directions:
1. Cut out the rectangles on the dark lines.
2. Cut the moon (crescent) and sun (circle) on the dark lines.
3. Color the rectangles on both sides with the color indicated.
4. Fold each rectangle in half on the dotted lines (word side facing in for the yellow rectangle).
5. Glue the solid black and blue halves together.
6. Glue the sun and moon to the yellow so that the yellow "shines" through. The pages should now flip from day to night.
7. Place a stretched cotton ball "cloud" on the solid blue piece. Place some star stickers on the solid black piece.

Options: (1) Use the rectangles on page 21 as patterns. Complete the activity using blue, black, and yellow construction paper. (2) Use blue, black, and yellow paper that is suitable for duplication. Duplicate enough rectangles of each suggested color for each pattern.

Song and Prayer

A hymn is a prayer set to music
And oh, how very nice
That when we use our sweet gift of song,
It's like we're praying—twice!

St. Augustine once said, "To sing is to pray twice." What does this mean? By adding the gift of song we add to the prayer and connect to others around us who may also be singing and enjoying our song. (Directions on page 24.)

Song and Prayer

Special Materials Needed:

• yarn

Directions:

1. Cut out the music notes on page 23.
2. Tell the name of your favorite songs from church. (Help the children by playing a recording of different church songs they may have heard.)
3. Print the name of your favorite song on the music note.

Additional Activities:

• Poke a hole in the top corners of the music notes. String a colorful piece of yarn through the holes and hang it on a bulletin board or around a prayer table.
• For young children, glue the music notes onto craft sticks. Have each child hold a stick and wave it as the class sings the church songs together. Also, let the students wave their music notes at a children's Mass while songs are sung.

The Door

The classic picture of Jesus standing outside the door preparing to knock is a powerful image. Of course, if you have seen this piece of art you know that there is no handle on the door. Therefore, Jesus cannot come in unless you open the door from inside. Jesus knocks, but we must be open to him.

How can you let Jesus into your life?

Directions:

1. Cut out the church and door along the dark lines.
2. Glue the left side of the door to the dark line on the church picture.
3. Think about what is missing on the door. (The handle.)
4. Draw a handle on the door that shows that you want to open the door and allow Jesus in.
5. Draw yourself inside the door, ready to greet Jesus.

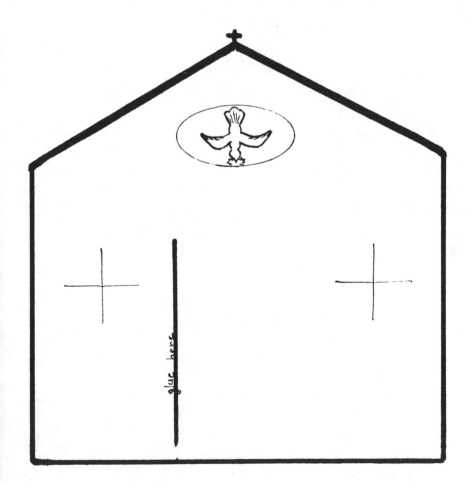

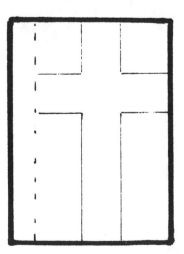

The Door

Additional Activities:

- Show the children a picture of "Jesus at the Door." There are many renditions available on the Internet.
- Share scripture verses in which Jesus refers to himself as the door or gate. For example: "knock, and the door will be opened for you . . . everyone who knocks will have the door opened" (Mt 7:7-8) and "I am the gate. Anyone who enters through me will be safe" (Jn 10:9).
- Ask: "What are some ways you can let Jesus into your life?"

Morning Prayer

In this busy world in which we live, it is easy to start the morning in a state of frenzy. Our morning clock seems to accelerate, moving too fast, and before we know it we are rushing, hollering, and scooting everyone out the door—too often we have started our day with a sense of panic.

How much more joyful it would be to start our day with a morning prayer. Our morning should be a new beginning; it should be sanctified and blessed.

Perhaps a small morning prayer on the refrigerator, bulletin board or framed beside the door would help us to stop, think, and begin the day with prayer.

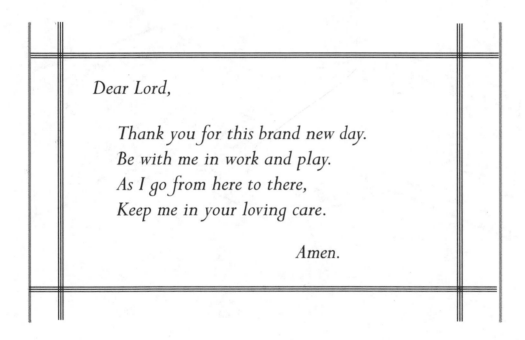

Dear Lord,

Thank you for this brand new day.
Be with me in work and play.
As I go from here to there,
Keep me in your loving care.

Amen.

Special Materials Needed:
- 3" x 5" index cards
- colored paper

Directions:
1. Create a short prayer, find another prayer you like, or use the prayer above. Neatly print the prayer on a 3" x 5" card.
2. Glue the card to a bright-colored construction paper border.
3. Take the prayer home and put it on your refrigerator. Recite it daily.

Kinds of Prayers

There are many ways to talk to God. There are many different kinds of prayers. Are your prayers usually "asking" prayers? Do you sometimes say "thank you" prayers? Are your prayers always the same kind?

Most children understand asking and thank you prayers. Explain that some of our prayers say, "Amen! Yes! I agree" as a way to acknowledge God's greatness. The "Great Amen" is a prayer like this. We also pray to seek reconciliation with God and other people.

Ask the children to think about all the ways we pray.

Special Materials Needed:
- 6" x 18" strips of paper

Directions:
1. Fold the strips of paper in half, then in half again (see above).
2. Open to reveal the four boxes.
3. Print a heading in each box to designate a different kind of prayer; for example, Asking Prayer, Thank You Prayer, The Great Amen, Help Me to Understand Prayer, Asking Forgiveness Prayer. Or you may be able to name a specific prayer they know and write the name of the prayer in the box under the heading (e. g., for an Asking Forgiveness Prayer you can print the words of an Act of Contrition you know).
4. Illustrate each box in whatever way you choose.

2

Liturgy

Liturgy means "public prayer."

Mass is a communal celebration, a coming together in prayer. In the Mass we reenact Christ's sacrifice for us on the cross and celebrate his winning of our salvation.

We are a church community. While it is true that we are a diverse mixture of people with different lives, backgrounds, and cultures, when we gather together in prayer we celebrate the one, blessed, and universal commemoration of sacrifice and salvation offered to us by Jesus Christ. We are one in Christ and are called on to take the good news from our liturgy and share it with others.

These lessons, projects, and crafts help us to answer the charge we are given at the conclusion of Mass, "Go forth to love and serve the Lord."

Vessels and Vestments

One of the advantages of my upbringing was that I had a familiarity with the sacred vessels and vestments used at Mass. Words like *paten, tabernacle*, and *cruets* were common to us. We understood that there were special items used at Mass because it was a time Jesus became present to us in the blessed bread and wine. We also could identify and name the priest's vestments; his chasuble, alb, and stole, for example.

It was also not uncommon for us as children to "play Mass." It seemed natural to pattern our play after a central part of our upbringing. To this day I have the green carnival glass that we dubbed "the chalice." Each time I look at it I see the doughy circles of bread we fashioned from a single piece of white bread that we flattened. I remember making the "hosts" with mother's orange hole-maker. (I'm not sure this kitchen device still exists, but my memories do!)

Recently I mentioned "playing Mass" to another adult Catholic. He too recalled "playing Mass" as one of his favorite childhood activities and confessed that he even had neighborhood children from other religions taking part. When I seemed surprised he admitted that he had been more ingenious with the "hosts" and used white candy wafers.

One of the reasons we felt so comfortable "playing Mass" is that we were familiar with the items used at Mass. Ask a priest to come into your classroom with some of the sacred vessels and vestments and explain their use. Or, take your children to the sacristy itself so that they will be able to view up close these important elements that are used at liturgy.

The Chasuble

A chasuble is the big-sleeved vestment the priest wears over the alb at Mass. The color of the chasuble represents a special season or special time in the church year. These colors are explained on the reverse side of this page. Notice the color of the vestments the next time you are at Mass. Do you know what season of the church year you are in? (Directions on back.)

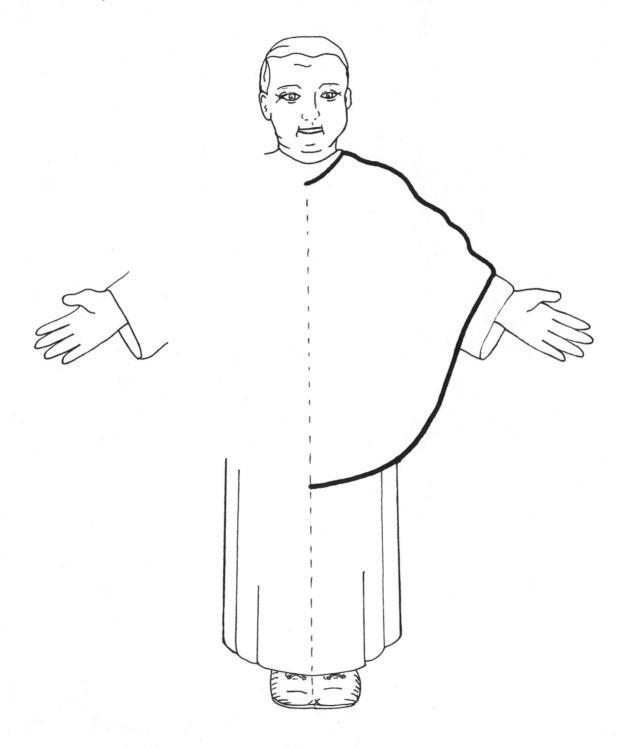

The Chasuble

Special Materials Needed:
- 6" x 6" squares of construction paper (in whichever color you wish to make the chasuble; see below)

Directions:
1. Fold the priest on the dotted center line.
2. Cut on the bold line and open.
3. Lightly glue the construction paper behind the priest so that the color shows through.

Additional Activities:
- Talk about the colors of the vestment using the guide below.
- Have a priest visit the classroom and talk about the colors of the vestments.
- Have the children draw the outline of a stole around the neck of the priest over the chasuble.

Green:
Ordinary Time

White:
Easter, Christmas
Season
Special feasts

Violet:
Lent, Advent,
Masses for the dead

Red:
Palm Sunday, Good
Friday, Pentecost
Feasts of Apostles
and Martyrs

Rose:
Third Sunday in Advent
(Gaudete Sunday)
Fourth Sunday in Lent (Laetare
Sunday)

My Church Photo Album

Most of the time Mass is celebrated in a church. We also know that Mass can be said anywhere if need be. Many times while people are saving the money to build a church, services are held in cafeterias, gymnasiums, lecture halls and the like. The parish community is happy when they finally have a special building of their own where they can gather. We are happy to have a building called a church. A church is our special place. A church is a wonderful, holy building that belongs to all of us. It is the house of God.

As a church community we care for our church and the buildings and the grounds around us, just as we care for our individual family homes. Think of places and things around our church building and grounds that hold a special meaning.

Have the children make a "photo" album showing the places at your church and surrounding grounds that are special to you. (Directions on back.)

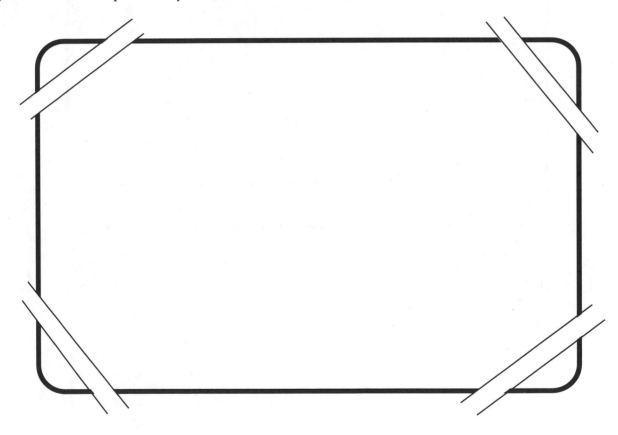

My Church Photo Album

Special Materials Needed:

- photos of your parish church and grounds (optional)

Directions:

1. Using these "photo" pages, draw pictures of your church and its surroundings.
2. Include some real photographs if they are available.

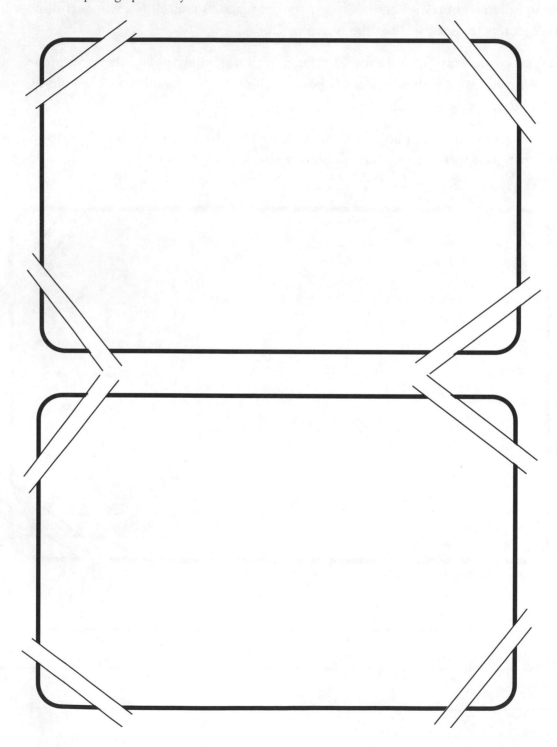

Two Main Parts of the Mass

Very young children may not be able to know the terms for the two main parts of the Mass—the *Liturgy of the Word* and the *Liturgy of the Eucharist*—but they can comprehend the importance of observing and becoming active participants at Mass. They can appreciate that the first part of the Mass centers around the word of God and that the second part centers around the consecration of the bread and wine. (Directions on the reverse side.)

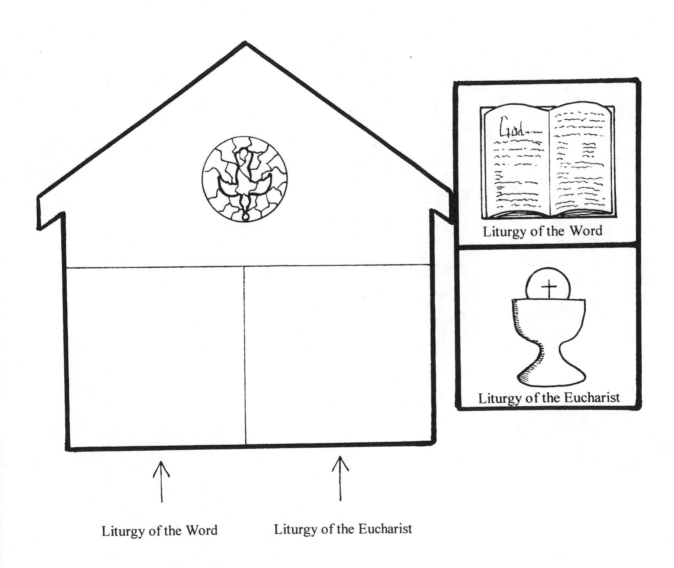

Liturgy of the Word

Liturgy of the Eucharist

Liturgy of the Word   Liturgy of the Eucharist

Two Main Parts of the Mass

Directions:

1. Cut out the outline of the church on the dark outside line.
2. Cut out and glue in place on the church the Liturgy of the Word and Liturgy of the Eucharist squares in the correct order in which they occur.

Additional Activities:

- Use a missal to take the children through the Mass while explaining the various parts.
- As you explain the division of the service, use the following simple hand motions to reinforce what you are saying. Have the students copy your motions.
  1. We say hello. (Wave slightly.)
  2. Liturgy of the Word. (Open and close your hands like a book.)
  3. Liturgy of the Eucharist. (Look heavenward, reach your hands up and bring them down in a praying motion, then motion receiving the Eucharist.)
  4. Go forth sharing. (Extend hands outward.)

Liturgy of the Word

Visualizing the various parts of the Liturgy of the Word helps us to see how the readings fit together, building up to the Gospel. This activity helps the children to learn the correct sequence of the Liturgy of the Word. (Directions are on the reverse side.)

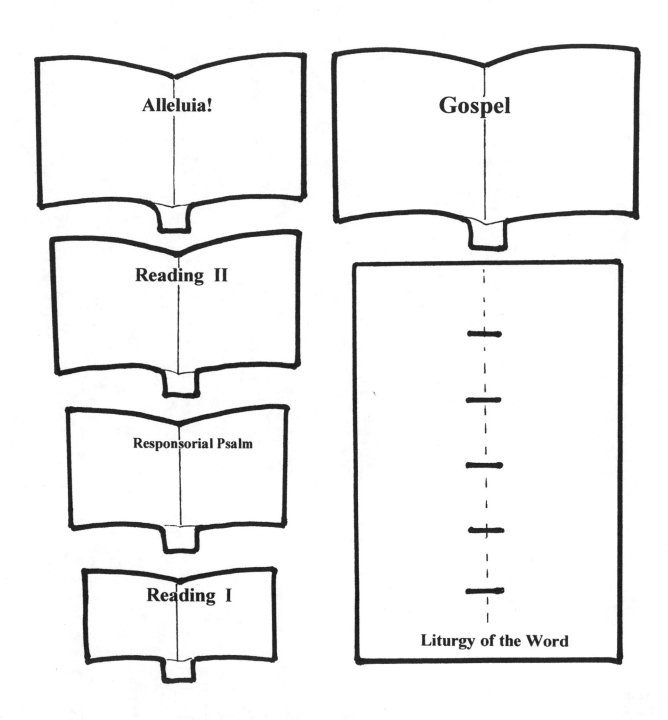

Liturgy of the Word

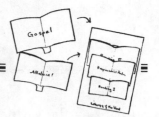

Directions:

1. Color each part of the Liturgy of the Word.
2. Cut them out on the dark lines.
3. Color and cut the part labeled Liturgy of the Word. Fold it in half on the dotted line. Cut small slits on the black lines. Open.
4. Insert the pieces into the slits from front to back. Go from the smallest on the bottom to the largest on the top. Glue or tape in place from the back, if necessary.
5. Stand the pieces up.

Additional Activity:

• Have the children memorize the sequence of readings of the Liturgy of the Word.

Liturgy of the Eucharist

At the time of the presentation of gifts, the Mass moves from the Liturgy of the Word to the Liturgy of the Eucharist. This is the most sacred time of the Mass. This activity helps the children learn how the Liturgy of the Eucharist progresses. (Directions are on the reverse side.)

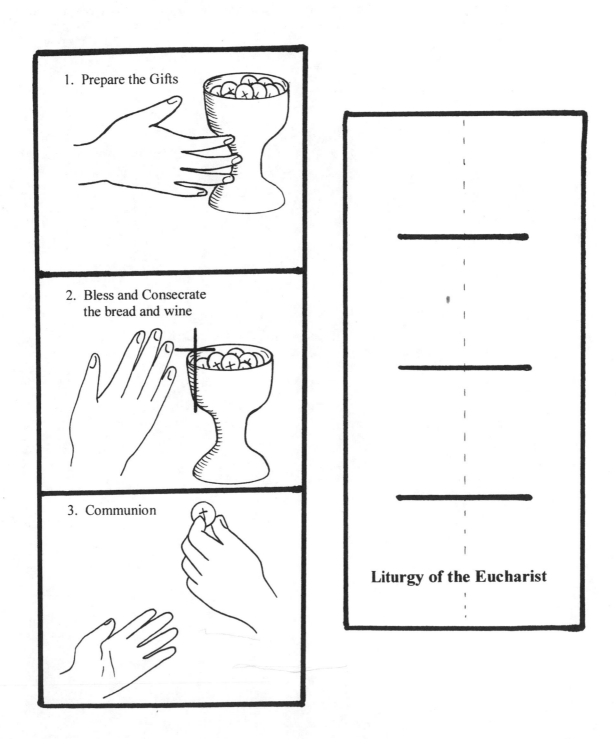

1. Prepare the Gifts

2. Bless and Consecrate the bread and wine

3. Communion

Liturgy of the Eucharist

Liturgy of the Eucharist

Directions:

1. Color all of the pieces, including the strip that says "Liturgy of the Eucharist."
2. Cut out all of the pieces.
3. Fold the Liturgy of the Eucharist strip on the line and carefully snip on the small lines. Open partially.
4. Insert the pieces into the slits so that they stand up.

Additional Activity:

• Help the children memorize the parts of the Liturgy of the Eucharist. Remove one of the pieces and have them guess which one is missing.

Gospel Preparation

Just prior to the priest or deacon reading the gospel, we cross ourselves three times. We curl our fingers and place our thumb upright. Then, we use our thumb to cross our forehead, lips, and heart. It is important for children to realize that the reading that takes place after this preparation is so important that we stand for it, listen to it, and then pay close attention as the priest or deacon explains the gospel and other readings in his homily. We, too, hear the good news of Jesus, speak it to others, and share the love of the gospel to all we meet. (Directions on reverse.)

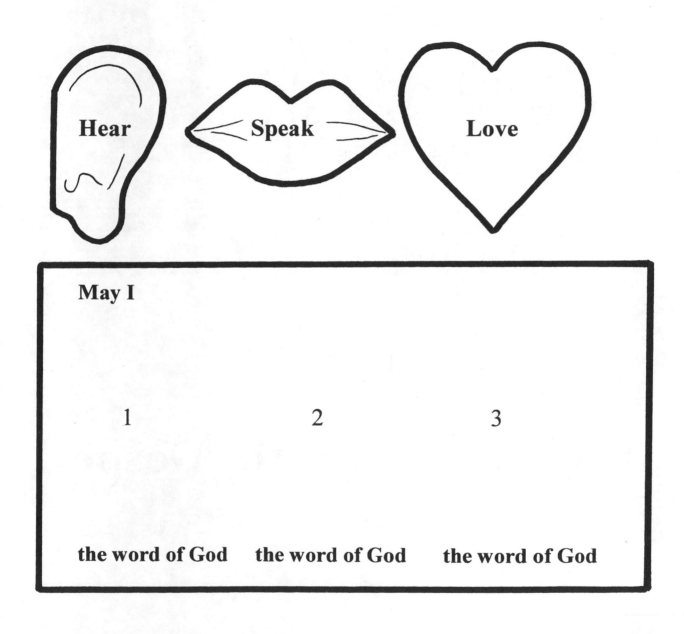

Hear　　**Speak**　　**Love**

May I

1　　　　2　　　　3

the word of God　**the word of God**　**the word of God**

Directions:

1. Cut out the "May I" rectangle.
2. Cut out the three separate pieces: ear, lips, and heart.
3. Glue the pieces on the 1, 2, and 3 in the proper order.

Additional Activity:

- Have the students read the words as they practice making a small cross on their forehead, lips, and heart.

Preparation for the Gospel

The Evangelists: Matthew, Mark, Luke, and John

The gospels come from the New Testament and the writings of the four evangelists. As a child, I was told a little poem that helped me remember the names of the evangelists who collected the stories and wrote so lovingly about Jesus and his life on earth.

We had a little holy water font at the entrance of the bedroom my sister and I shared. We would sprinkle a little holy water on our bed and recite, "Matthew, Mark, Luke, and John, bless the bed that I sleep on."

Today we seldom have holy water fonts in our homes, but it is still good to remember that the four evangelists formed the core of the good news about Jesus that we share with others. (Directions on the reverse.)

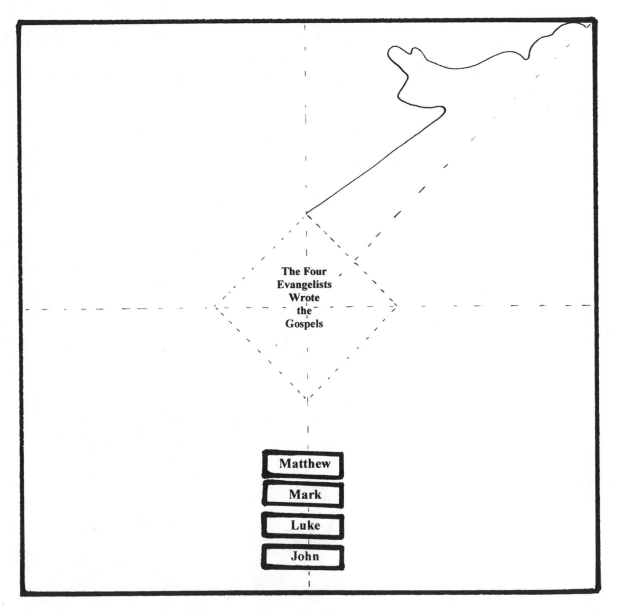

The Four
Evangelists
Wrote
the
Gospels

Matthew

Mark

Luke

John

The Evangelists: Matthew, Mark, Luke, and John

Directions:

1. Cut the square on the dark line.
2. Carefully fold the page in half, and then in half again, with the evangelist showing.
3. Carefully fold the page on the diagonal forming a triangle so that only the half figure shows.
4. Hold on the fold and cut out the evangelist figure. (For younger children, have an adult cut the figure and allow the child to open it.)
5. Open. (Color a face and clothing on each of the evangelists.)
6. Cut out the names of each evangelist, and glue them on the figures. Or, write the names on the figures.
7. Fold on the center dotted line. Connect the hands together with glue or tape.

Additional Activity:

• Sample the four gospels with the children. For example, compare how each evangelist tells or omits the same event from Jesus' life.

"Peace Be With You" Doves

After the Our Father at Mass, we greet each other with a sign of peace symbolized by a hand-shake, hug, or kiss. Children should learn that the sign of peace is more than an automatic response. First, the priest offers us all the sign of peace. We reciprocate. Then we offer peace to one another. Our sign of peace shows that we are part of a community, a family of God, and that we want God's peace and love to be with all people. (Directions on reverse.)

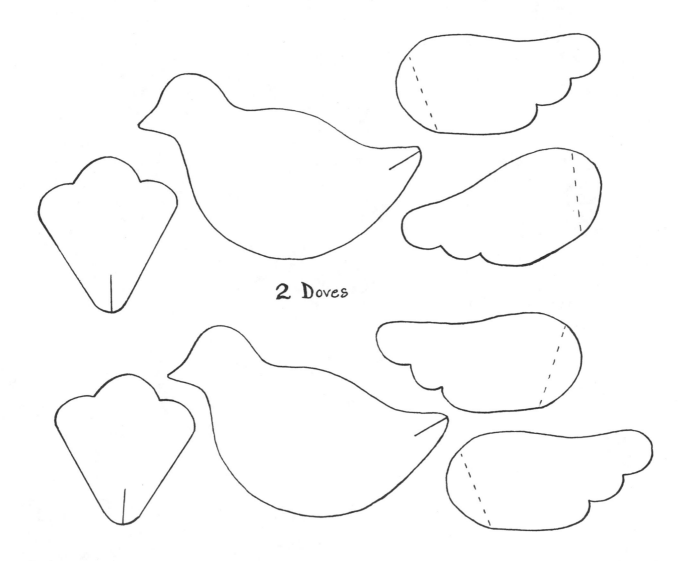

2 Doves

"Peace Be With You" Doves

Special Materials Needed:

*   stapler
*   single hole punch
*   string or yarn

Directions:

1. Cut out all of the parts of the two doves: bodies, wings, and tails.
2. Place the wings on each side of the body. Staple in place.
3. Slide the tail in place.
4. Hole punch eye, if desired.

Additional Activities:

*   Hang the dove with string or yarn from the ceiling.
*   Give the peace dove to someone and offer that person the "sign of peace."
*   Place a green sprig in the dove's beak.

Note: The peace doves also make lovely ornaments for Christmas trees. As a frugal young wife our first Christmas tree consisted of red bows and these white doves. It will always be a memory of one of the loveliest Christmas trees ever—our tree of peace.

The Last Supper: The First Eucharist

The Last Supper was also the first Eucharist. When Jesus took the bread and cup of wine, blessed them, and offered them to his disciples he instituted the same ritual that we participate in at each Mass. The scriptures tell us:

> Then he took bread, and when he had given thanks, he broke it and gave it to them, saying, "This is my body given for you; do this in remembrance of me." He did the same with the cup after supper, and said, "This cup is the new covenant in my blood poured out for you" (Luke 22:19-20).

With these words Jesus established the Eucharist and called on us to respect his words and actions in remembrance of him. (Directions on following page.)

The Last Supper

...do this in remembrance of me.

The Last Supper: The First Eucharist

Special Materials Needed:
- scraps of cloth
- glitter

Directions:
1. Cut the dark outer line of the Last Supper.
2. Color faces, hair, beards, scarves, etc. on the apostles.
3. Color the picture.
4. Add scraps of cloth to the clothing.
5. Add glitter to the coronal above Christ's head.
6. Fold "The Last Supper" on the dotted lines to make the scene stand.

Additional Activity:
- Read the different gospel versions of the institution of the Eucharist (Matthew 26:26-28, Mark 14:22-24, Luke 22:19-20). Note both their similarities and differences. Discuss.

3

The Bible

The Bible is the sacred book of Christians. Its teachings span all generations.

It is important that we instill in children an early appreciation for the sacred word. We can do this in several ways.

Instilling a love for the Bible early on will lead to a greater understanding and appreciation of the scriptures when the child grows.

The activities in this chapter are designed to encourage interest and reading of the Bible, both Old Testament and New Testament.

Old/New Testament Match

As children become more familiar with the Bible, they will distinguish between the stories and texts of the Old and New Testaments. This easy match game will help the children to learn that the Old Testament is a memorial to God's early people, that it lays the groundwork for the saving works of Jesus.

Remind the students that any story that tells about Jesus or is a parable or story told by Jesus is found in the New Testament. The following game is designed to promote a comfort level and familiarity with the Bible. Children may work in small groups with bibles for reference to insure success.

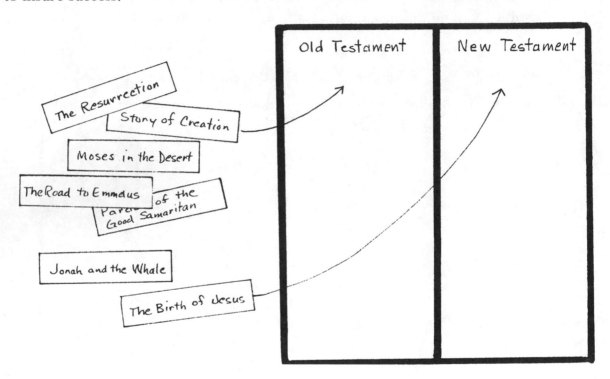

Directions:
1. Divide a blackboard or large piece of poster board into two sections. Mark one side *Old Testament* and the other *New Testament*.
2. Hold up cards with words, phrases, or titles on them one at a time (e.g., Jonah and the Whale, The Letters of Paul to the Romans, The Parable of the Lamp, and The Visit of the Magi). If the group is more proficient, hold up names of books of the Bible (e.g., Genesis, Exodus, Matthew, and Acts).
3. Call on students to put each word, phrase, or title under the correct column.

Additional Activity:
- Divide the class into two teams. Team 1 names a Bible story or Bible book title. Team 2 confers and then decides in which column to place the story or title. Award one point for each correct answer.

Rainbow Streamers

In the Bible, a rainbow is a sign of God's healing. We think of a rainbow as a warm, comforting symbol, and a sign of a connection between heaven and earth. The rainbow is a sign of joy, a sign of God's love. Some of the Bible references where a rainbow is mentioned are:

Genesis 9:12-17

Sirach 43:11-12

Ezekiel 1:28

Read the entire story of Noah from Genesis 6-9 and the other verses that mention a rainbow as a way to preview this project. (Directions on the reverse side.)

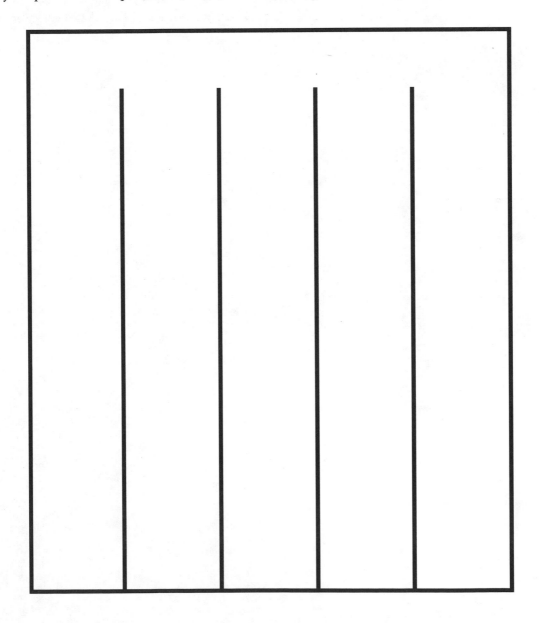

Rainbow Streamers

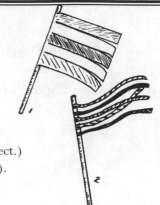

Special Materials Needed:
- craft sticks or straws
- colored tissue strips or yarn (optional)

Directions:
1. Color each strip a different color of the rainbow.
2. Cut out the rectangle on the solid black outer line.
3. Cut each strip from the outer edge to the stopping point. (Do not disconnect.)
4. Glue or tape the connecting strip to the end of a craft stick or straw (fig. 1).

Additional Activities:
- Instead of using the pattern, have the children cut out colored tissue strips or yarn in rainbow colors and glue the streamers or yarn to a craft stick or straw (fig. 2).
- Call on the children to sing and dance around the room to a joyous song while waving the rainbow streamers.
- Read the story of Noah's Ark (Gen 6-9). Have the children wave the streamers when the rainbow is mentioned.

A Psalm Tree

As a child it made quite an impression on me when a teacher suggested that the Blessed Mother might have sung the Psalms to the Christ Child to soothe him to sleep. The Psalms are hymns of praise to God that are included in the Old Testament. I marveled to think that those same beautiful, little verses being read to me had been read nearly two thousand years ago to Jesus. I listened with a new appreciation. I wondered if Jesus understood all of the words and meanings or if he too struggled to understand what was being taught.

While many of the Psalm verses are beyond a child's comprehension, there are also many verses easily understood by children. For example, Psalm 19 begins, "The heavens declare the glory of God." Psalm 34 starts, "I will bless the Lord at all times; his praise shall be ever in my mouth." A glance through the book of Psalms will reveal many other verses that are appropriate for children. (Directions are on page 54.)

A Psalm Tree

Special Materials Needed:

- bare tree limb
- coffee can with pebbles
- yarn or string

Directions:

1. Choose one or more psalms you like.
2. Print favorite verses from the psalms on each bible outline or draw a picture to describe what the verses mean to you. (Older children may wish to write and draw using both sides of the book.)
3. Hole punch the top of each book. Lace with yarn or string and tie. Hang the verses from a branch that is placed in a tin can filled with pebbles to make a "Psalm Tree."

Floating Noah's Ark

One of the classic Old Testament stories is Noah's Ark. Read the story from Genesis 6-9. The activity asks you to make an ark and then put it in a sink of water. When the water moves back and forth, you will see how the ark would have protected Noah and his family. (Directions on reverse.)

Floating Noah's Ark

Special Materials Needed:
- empty foam egg carton
- photos of animals cut from magazines (optional)
- permanent markers
- glue
- scissors

Fig. 1

Fig. 2

Directions:
1. Color and cut out the pictures on the previous page. Or, cut out some small-sized photos of animals from magazines.
2. Close the egg carton. Turn it upside down (see fig. 1).
3. Make a large I-shaped cut on one of the cups to make a window that will open and close (see fig. 2). Repeat the cut on several of the cups.
4. Glue the pictures inside the windows (or for younger children, glue on the outside of an uncut cup).
5. Glue the egg carton closed.

Additional Activities:
- Have the children draw some of their own animals.
- Provide a sink-full of water. Have the children put their arks in the water and move the water back and forth with their hands. Open the drain to depict the end of the flood.

Jonah and the Whale

The story of Jonah and the Whale is a favorite with children and adults alike. While children may be fascinated with the concept of a huge whale, we know that the symbolism of the story is of the essence. The fact that Jonah was in the whale for three days mirrors the three days Jesus was in the tomb. Jonah, fully restored, was released from the whale at the end of his entombment, foreshadowing the resurrection. This story teaches the universality of God's love. Too, this story shows the importance of listening to the Lord and following the commandments.

Read the story from the Bible or tell this narrative:

From the **Book of Jonah**

God spoke to Jonah. "Up! Go to Nineveh. Tell them that their wickedness has forced itself upon me." Jonah did not want to go to Nineveh and tell the people to mend their ways. So, Jonah ran away. He found a ship going to Tarshish, paid his fare, and boarded it. But God sent a hurricane at sea and the ship seemed ready to be destroyed. All of the sailors began praying to their gods. Jonah was down in the hold of the ship, sleeping. A sailor went to him and said, "What do you mean by sleeping? Get up! Call on your God!"

As the storm raged on the sailors decided to cast lots and find out who was to blame for bringing them bad luck. The lot pointed to Jonah. The sailors went to Jonah. He confessed that he was running away from God. Jonah replied, "Take me and throw me into the sea, and then it will calm down for you. I know it is my fault that this great storm has struck you." The sailors didn't want to throw Jonah into the sea and so they rowed harder. But still the stormy seas grew rougher and rougher. The sailors asked for God's forgiveness as they hesitantly threw Jonah into the raging waters. The seas calmed.

On God's command a great fish swam by and scooped Jonah up into its mouth. Jonah remained in the belly of the fish for three days and three nights. From the belly of the fish Jonah prayed to Yahweh, his God. Yahweh spoke to the fish and on the third day the fish deposited Jonah onto dry land.

Jonah set out and went to Nineveh in obedience to the word of God. When he got to Nineveh he preached to the people and the people believed in God and began to mend their ways. When the king of Nineveh heard this he too began fasting and commanded that everyone in the kingdom denounce evil ways and violent behavior.

God spared the people of Nineveh. They listened and they were saved.

Jonah

(Directions on the reverse side.)

The Bible

57

Jonah and the Whale

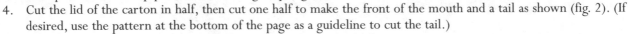

Special Materials Needed:
- egg carton with a dozen cups
- baggy ties (2)
- black permanent marker
- hole punch

Directions:
1. Open the egg carton and cut off the top.
2. Cut the cup part into two six-cup pieces.
3. Hole punch the six-cup piece at the cut edge top (fig. 1).
4. Cut the lid of the carton in half, then cut one half to make the front of the mouth and a tail as shown (fig. 2). (If desired, use the pattern at the bottom of the page as a guideline to cut the tail.)
5. Hole punch the top so that it will connect with the hole punched six-cup piece.
6. String a baggy tie through the holes (fig. 3).
7. Draw eyes on the great fish.
8. Color and cut out Jonah and put him in the whale.

Additional Activity:
- Have the children draw their own Jonah to place in the whale.

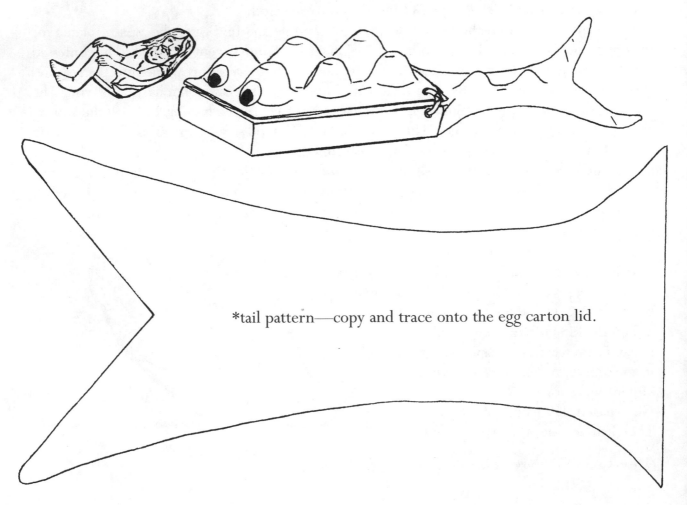

*tail pattern—copy and trace onto the egg carton lid.

Footsteps of Jesus

Jesus' words and teachings changed people forever. Jesus is the most influential person who ever lived. He is God Made Flesh. Yet, Jesus' public life lasted only three years, and he never traveled very far from home. Jesus did most of his preaching and teaching on foot as he walked the land.

We can explore maps of Jesus' time to find out more about where he lived. We know where Jesus was born. We know where he grew up. Also, we know where he performed his first miracle and where he did much of his teaching. A map also shows where Jesus was crucified, died, and buried.

> Jesus was born in **Bethlehem** and lived in **Nazareth**.
> Jesus performed his first miracle at the wedding at **Cana**.
> Jesus traveled throughout **Galilee** and calmed the **Sea of Galilee**.
> Jesus preached at **Capernaum** and **Bethsaida**.
> Jesus traveled throughout **Judea** and walked with his disciples at **Emmaus** after his resurrection.

Directions:
1. Cut out one pair of sandals and glue them to a craft stick.
2. Use this like a pointer, moving the sandals from place to place. (see drawing above.)
3. Tell a friend about where Jesus lived and traveled.

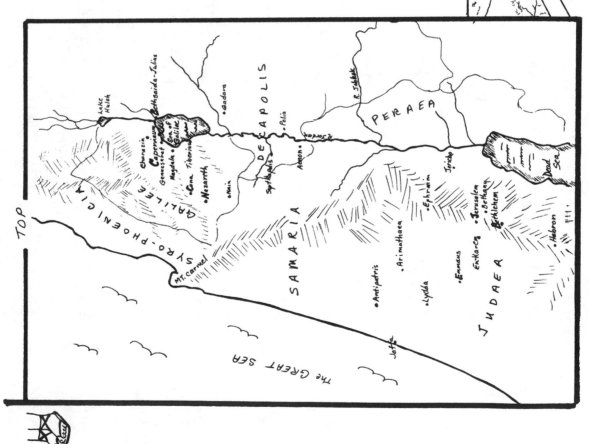

The Wedding at Cana

Jesus performed his first miracle at a wedding feast in Cana. This event is recorded in John 2:1-12. Jesus was at this wedding feast with his mother.

While they were at the feast, the wine ran out. Mary said, "They have no wine." Jesus asked what she wanted him to do. His time to do miracles had not yet come, he told her.

Still, Mary told the servants to do what Jesus asked. Jesus then told the servants to fill the six stone water jars standing nearby with water. He also told them to draw some water and take it to the head waiter. They obeyed. The head waiter tasted the water; it had turned into wine. The waiter called the bridegroom and said, "Everyone serves good wine first and the worse wine when the guests are well wined; but you have kept the best wine till now."

This activity helps the children reenact the first of Jesus' signs.

Special Materials Needed:
*   six clear plastic "glasses"
*   presweetened drink mix, preferably red in color
*   spoon

Directions:
1. Lay out the six clear plastic "glasses" in a row.
2. Fill all the glasses with water just as the servants were asked by Jesus to do. (Point out that this water will all be changed into a flavored drink by adding something to the water, but Jesus was able to change the water into wine by blessing it. What he did was a miracle.)
3. Slowly pour a few teaspoons of drink mix in each cup. Notice the water changing color.
4. Share the sweetened water with each other.

Additional Activity:
*   Discuss with the children how surprised and startled the guests, bridegroom, and others must have been when Jesus was able to change water into wine. Ask: "How do you think Mary felt?"

Loaves and Fishes

The Bible tells us about Jesus feeding the multitudes from a meager offering. All four of the evangelists recount miracles of Jesus feeding the people.

Read and note the similarities of the following accounts: Matthew 14:13-21, 15:32-39; Mark 6:30-44, 8:1-9; Luke 9:10-17; John 6:3-13.

In each story huge crowds follow Jesus. Jesus preaches to them. It is at mealtime when the crowds are hungry that the apostles ask what they should do. Jesus suggests feeding the people. The Apostles are at a loss since there are so many people and they have little or no money with which to buy food. Jesus asks what food is available and a small offering of loaves and fishes are brought to him. Jesus looks to heaven and blesses the food and tells the disciples to pass it out to all. Not only does everyone get their fill, there are many baskets left over.

Help children recognize the many ways God provides for our needs. (Directions on the reverse side.)

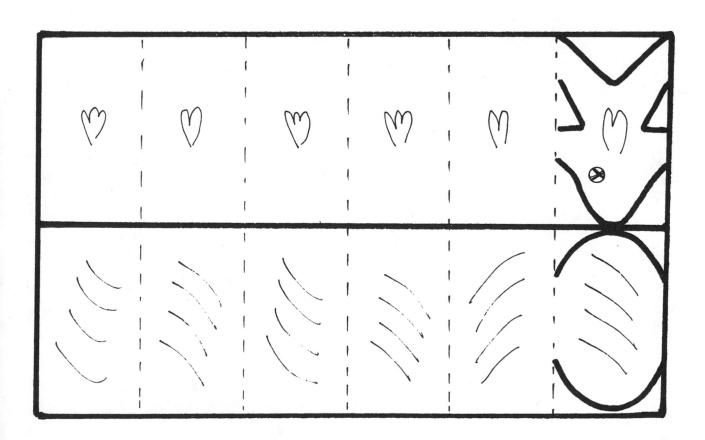

Loaves and Fishes

Special Materials Needed:
- brown lunch bag
- single hole punch

Directions:
1. Cut out the fish and bread rectangular pattern pieces on the dark outer lines.
2. Accordion fold the fish and bread strips on the dotted lines with the fish and loaf on the top, then cut along the dark lines to make fish and loaf shapes.
3. Hole punch the eye of the fish.
4. Cut a one-inch "basket" from the bottom of the lunch bag.
5. Tape the last fish and loaf to the basket.

Additional Activities:
- Read one of the stories on the multiplication of loaves and fishes from the Bible (see previous page).
- Discuss real-life ways that the children can help feed people in our midst who are hungry.

Let Your Light Shine

Jesus is the "light of the world." Jesus brought us out of darkness and into the light of salvation. Jesus is not only the light of the world, he calls us to be light for others too. He said, "I am the light of the world; anyone who follows me will not be walking in the dark, but will have the light of life." And Jesus adds, "You are light for the world. A city built on a hill-top cannot be hidden. No one lights a lamp to put it under a tub; they put it on the lamp-stand where it shines for everyone in the house. In the same way your light must shine in people's sight, so that, seeing your good works, they may give praise to your Father in heaven" (Mt 5:14-16).

This activity will remind children to let their light shine! (Directions on page 64.)

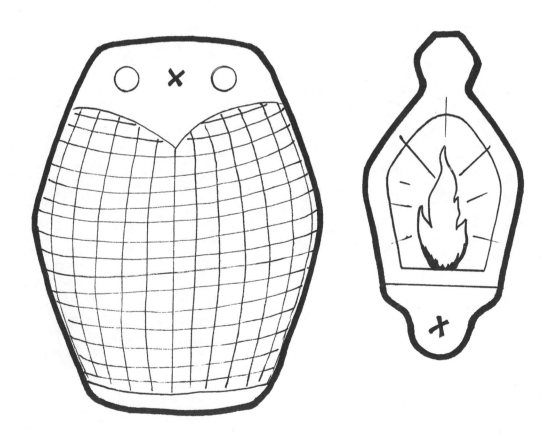

Let Your Light Shine

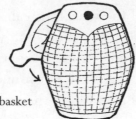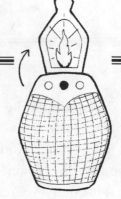

Special Materials Needed:
- brass fastener (brad)

Directions:
1. Color the pieces.
2. Cut out the lamp and basket pieces.
3. Put the brass fastener through the "X" on the basket and then through the "X" on the lamp piece.
4. Slide the light behind the basket. As you say, "Let your light shine on me," flip the lamp out from behind the basket.

Additional Activities:
- Discuss good works we can do to make our *light shine*. (For example: Visit the sick or elderly. Fill food baskets, collect cans, newspapers, etc., for recycling drives. Help a neighbor. Watch a younger brother or sister for our parents.)
- Discuss other ways we interact with people that make our *light shine*. (For example: controlling our tempers, talking respectfully, avoiding gossip, etc.)

Jesus Loves the Little Children

We know that children hold a special place in Jesus' heart.

When the apostles were arguing about whom among them was the greatest, Jesus placed a child before them and said, "Anyone who welcomes a little child such as this in my name welcomes me" (Mk 9:36-37).

Another time when some children were being brought to Jesus for a blessing and the disciples knew Jesus was tired, the disciples tried to turn the children away. Jesus stopped them saying, "Let the little children come to me; do not stop them; for it is to such as these that the kingdom of God belongs. In truth I tell you, anyone who does not welcome the kingdom of God like a little child will never enter it" (Mk 10:13-16).

Jesus loves the little children!

(Directions on reverse side.)

The Bible

Jesus Loves the Little Children

Directions:

1. Color the pieces.
2. Cut out the outline of the child.
3. Draw facial features and clothing on the child outline.
4. Cut out the picture of Jesus on the dark outer line.
   (Carefully cut around Jesus' arm; bend the arm on the folding
   lines as if Jesus is putting his arm around the little child.)

Additional Activities:

- Put a photo of the child's face on the cutout.
- Have the children discuss what they might say to Jesus if they were actually among the crowds of people who came to listen to the Lord's preaching.

Angels and Archangels

Angels are a special part of our faith. They are special messengers from God, created with a soul but without a body. In the Bible, there are many references to angels. The church teaches that angels are *pure spirits* created by God. Archangels are messengers who spoke directly to human beings. The archangels are Michael, Gabriel, and Raphael. We can think of angels and archangels as God's helpers. (Directions on reverse.)

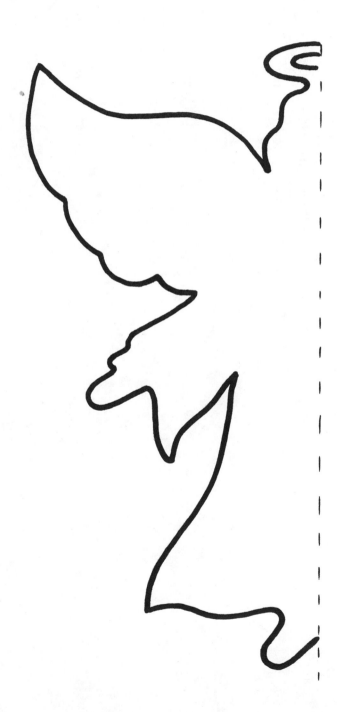

Angels and Archangels

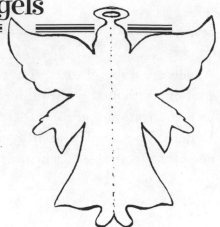

Directions:

1. Fold the pattern on the dotted center line.
2. Hold the fold and cut on the dark outside line.
3. Open the pattern.
4. Decorate.

Additional Activities:

- Tape a thread to the back of the angel to make it fly.
- Tape the angel to a craft stick to make a puppet.
- Use a flashlight to cast an angel silhouette on the wall.

4

Legends and Lore

A legend is a story handed down from earlier times that most people believe has roots in history, though its historical context may not be able to be verified. Lore refers to accumulated facts, traditions, and beliefs about a particular subject. Our religion is filled with elements of both legend and lore that help to explain religious practices that have become part of the fabric of our lives.

Some of the legends and lore of Christianity have roots in non-Christian traditions. The date of Christmas, for example, was placed near the winter solstice, the Roman celebration of the "Unconquered Sun." Soon Christians were celebrating December 25 as "Christ Mass," a day for recalling that Jesus' birth brought permanent light into a dark world.

Legends and lore associated with our Christian faith appeal to children and adults alike. They need not be explained in word for word detail. The activities in this section only provide a brief introduction (though more reference information is provided in the Endnotes section).

The beauty of legends and lore lives on in our desire to share our faith, hope, and love with our children and with the rest of the world.

How the Ladybug Got Its Name

In the Middle Ages most people raised their own food. Many people were very poor. If anything happened to their crops, they would suffer greatly since there was little money to buy food from anyone else. One year a terrible thing happened. The people noticed bugs on their crops. More and more bugs came. Aphids and other insects were destroying many of the plants. The people were very sad and didn't know what to do. Their food would soon be gone.

The people had a great devotion to the Blessed Mother. They began to pray. They asked Mary to send them help, to save the crops, and to destroy the bad bugs. They prayed and prayed. Soon they saw small shiny red bugs with black dots appear on the plants. They looked again and realized these insects were good insects. These insects were eating the aphids and bad bugs! The crops were saved.

The people began to cheer and rejoice. They joyously praised the Blessed Mother and thanked her for sending the beautiful shiny red bugs. They began calling the saving insects "Our Lady's Bugs". The people were sure that Mary had answered their prayers. To this day, the ladybug is considered a sign of good fortune and joy in many countries of the world.
(Directions on reverse.)

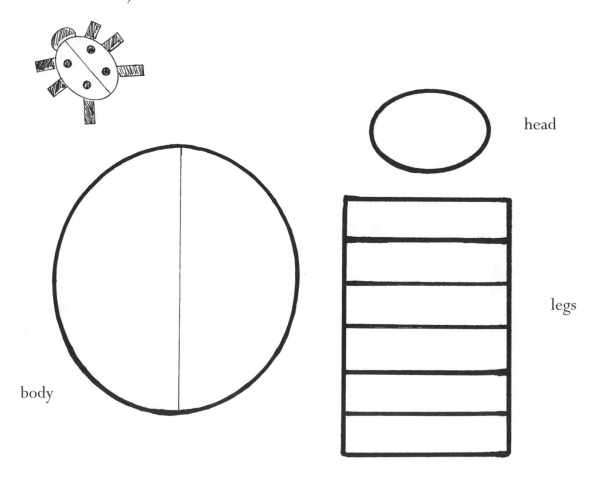

head

legs

body

How the Ladybug Got Its Name

Special Materials Needed:
- red and black construction paper(optional)
- single hole punch

Directions:
1. Color the ladybug's body red with black spots, its legs and head black.
2. Cut out the parts of the ladybug (legs, head, body).
3. Use black hole punch dots for spots on the ladybug's body.
4. Glue pieces in place.

Additional Activities:
- Share these fun facts about ladybugs:
  The two-spotted ladybug is *Adalia bipunctata*.
  The nine-spotted ladybug is *Coccinella novemnotata*.
  The ten-spotted ladybug is *Hippodamia convergens*.
  The Spanish word for ladybug is "Mariquita."
- After telling the "Story of the Ladybug," provide paper, brushes, and red and black paint and have the children paint pictures of ladybugs.
- Use the ladybug parts on page 71 as patterns for the children to make their own ladybugs from black and red construction paper.

Sand Dollar Treasure

The sand dollar is often thought of as a seashell. It is really a beautiful, flat sea urchin. When someone finds a sand dollar the first thing they usually do is examine it carefully. They hold it in their hands and study their newfound treasure.

It isn't too surprising that a long time ago a legend grew up around the sand dollar since it is so uniquely marked. The sand dollar became a sign of God's love and contained a message of the good news of Christ. Look closely at a sand dollar and you will understand how this legend came about. The urchin has five notches around its outside to represent the wounds to Christ's head by the crown of thorns and to his feet and hands by the nails. Another slit in the sand dollar represents the spear wound to Jesus' side made by the Roman soldier. One side of the urchin has a poinsettia etched in it to remind us of Christmastime. An Easter lily is on the other side; its center forms a star like the one seen by the shepherds. Finally, when the center is broken, five white doves are released to spread joy, goodwill, and peace.

The sand dollar forevermore is a gift for spreading the gospel.

(The directions are on page 74.)

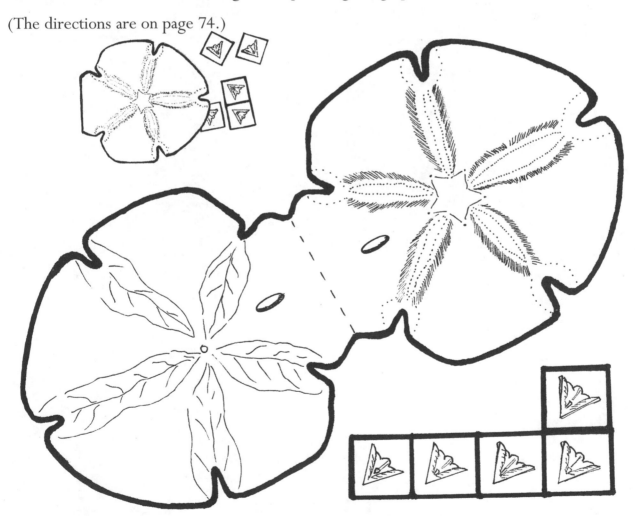

Sand Dollar Treasure

Directions:

1. Cut the sand dollar on the dark outside line.
2. Fold on the dotted line.
3. Trace the poinsettia, lily, and star if desired.
4. Glue together at the sides only to form a pocket. Leave an opening at the top.
5. Cut out the five little doves on the dark lines. When the glue is dry, slip the doves inside.

Additional Activity:

• If possible, bring in a sand dollar to display.

The Christmas Tree

There are several stories that suggest how the Christmas tree became part of our celebration of Christmas.

We can be fairly certain that the tradition began in Germany in the sixteenth century and German and English immigrants were the first people to introduce the Christmas tree to America. Prince Albert may have borrowed the custom from Germany and placed a Christmas tree in Windsor Castle in 1841, thus spreading the tradition to other parts of Europe.

Some people date the Christmas tree to an even earlier time, to a legend about St. Boniface in the eighth century. It is said that Boniface was walking through the forest and saw some men trying to cut down a tree to use as a stake in a human sacrifice. Boniface took the axe and cut the tree with one blow. The huge tree fell and split open. As it split a young fir tree sprang from its center. The branches pointed toward heaven. St. Boniface told the men that this was the Christ Child's tree, a holy tree. He instructed them to take fir trees into their homes, decorate the trees and surround them with gifts to remind them of God.

In any case, the Christmas tree is a symbol of Christ's everlasting love for us and represents the love and faith we have in Jesus. Its bows point upward to heaven, it stays green throughout the entire year, and its fragrance brings a sense of contentment and joy. (The directions are on the reverse.)

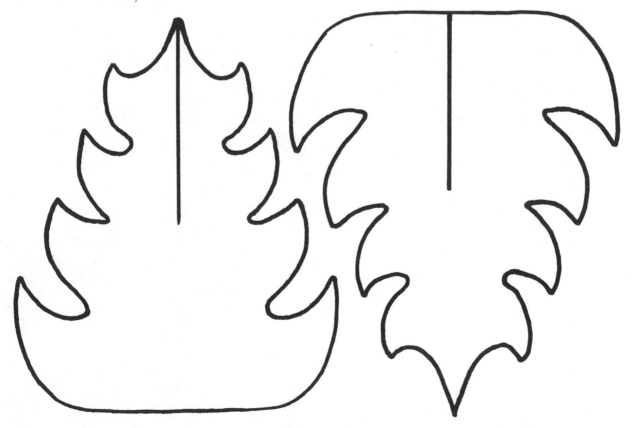

The Christmas Tree

Special Materials Needed:
* sticker stars, hole punch dots, yarn scraps, and other items for decorating a Christmas tree

Directions:
1. Use the trees as patterns for tracing on green construction paper—or color the trees green on all sides before cutting.
2. Cut out the tree patterns.
3. Carefully put the tree together at the slots. Tape in place if necessary.
4. Decorate the tree with sticker stars, hole punch dots, yarn scraps, and other items.

Additional Activity:
* Share the following information about Christmas trees with the children:

The first Christmas tree decorations were apples and lighted candles. The candles proved to be too dangerous and with the advent of the electric light, strings of lights were invented. Now trees could be put up earlier and enjoyed for a longer period of time. Apples proved to be too heavy and, therefore, "apples of glass" were made, thus producing the first glass ball ornaments. The reflective quality added a new dimension. Each year new and different decorations are produced, but the tradition of decorating the tree remains.

The Christmas Poinsettia

Of all the symbols of Christmas, the poinsettia flower is one of the most striking. Usually we think of the poinsettia as a bright red flower. Poinsettias can also have white and pink painted leaves. But, many people don't realize that the red, pink, or white leaves of the poinsettia are not really the flower part of the plant. The true flowers of the poinsettia are the little yellow center clusters. The rich beauty of the painted leaves suggests the uniqueness of this plant and has inspired this story:

> Once there was a little Mexican boy named Mario. Each Christmas Eve he watched as the people walked in procession to the church to take flowers to the Christ Child. Mario had no flowers and no money with which to buy them. One year he was kneeling outside the church crying because he had no flowers. A voice from a stone angel next to him whispered that he should pick some weeds and take them to Jesus. The boy thought the weeds weren't good enough for Jesus, but the angel told him that the simplest gifts, when given with love, are the most wonderful. He picked a handful of weeds and carried them to Jesus. As the boy placed the weeds at the Christ Child's feet, the leaves turned green and flame red and tiny blossoms like stars shone in the center. The humble weeds turned into the most beautiful flower and became a symbol of the Christmas season. Mexican tradition says that the plants are symbolic of the star of Bethlehem.

(Directions on reverse.)

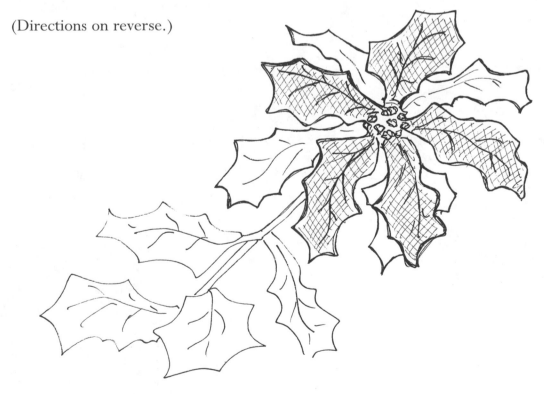

The Christmas Poinsettia

Special Materials Needed:
- red and green construction paper or tissue paper
- white glue with water (two parts glue/one part water)
- paintbrush
- white construction paper for background
- yellow construction paper
- single hole punch

Directions:
1. *Tear* red and green construction or tissue paper in 1" strips.
2. Carefully tear the end of the strips to make points.
3. Brush some of the glue mixture on the white paper.
4. Lay four or five of the green strips on the glue mixture so that they touch at the center and point outward. Then, coat each with more glue mixture.
5. Glue the red strips in a similar manner having them touch in the center. Continue coating each with more glue mixture.
6. Hole punch some yellow construction paper. Drop the dots in the center.

The Candy Cane

The candy cane is a delicious symbol of Christmas. There are many stories as to how the candy cane became a Christmas tradition. Some people believe that centuries ago the peppermint candy was made to be used as a sweet reward for children who were well behaved in church. Some say that the candy was a reward for children who learned their prayers.

Another story claims that the candy was invented in the seventeenth century and that the first canes were really just straight white sticks used for decorating Christmas trees. It is said that around the late 1600s, the choirmaster at the Cologne Cathedral convinced candy makers to bend the stick to symbolize the shepherd's crook. No one seems sure as to when the candy became red and white striped but in the early twentieth century the candy began appearing on Christmas cards this way. The wide red stripe is said to represent the sacrifice of Christ. Narrow red strips represent our sacrifices (good deeds and giving) and the white of the candy is a symbol of purity.

Now candy canes are available in many flavors, but the traditional flavor is peppermint. Peppermint is a member of the hyssop family, a medicinal herb used for cleansing that is mentioned in the Old Testament.

When a candy cane is broken, it reminds us that Christ's body was broken for us. As we share the peppermint we share in the sweetness of Christmas.

No matter what story we believe about the origin of the candy cane, it is most definitely a sweet treat and a lovely symbol of Christmas. (Directions on reverse.)

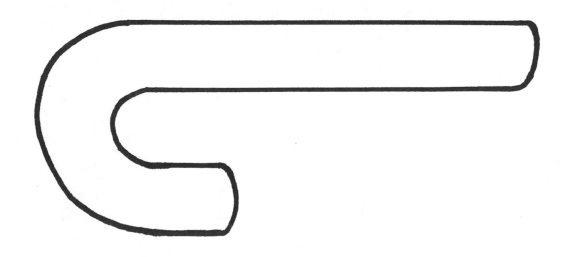

The Candy Cane

Special Materials Needed:
- white glue with water (two parts glue/one part water)
- red paint or red glitter
- toothpick or fine paintbrush

Directions:
1. Use the pattern from the previous page. Cut out a candy cane shape from white poster board for each child.
2. Place the cane on waxed paper.
3. Spread white glue completely on one side of the cane.
4. With a toothpick or small brush, slide a small amount of red paint or glitter across the glue to make stripes.
5. Allow to dry.

Additional Activities:
- Use red and white bendable straws that have an "elbow." Cut two straws at 4" each from the straight end. Pull and bend the accordion part of the straw to form a cane. Repeat with the second straw. Cross the canes and staple. Tie a ribbon and bow at the staple to hide it.
- Share real candy canes with the children while they are working.
- Bring in solid white candy canes and allow the children to drape shiny red ribbon on them to remind them of Christ's sacrifice. Encourage them to present the cane as a gift to a family member.

The Easter Egg

We're familiar with receiving chocolate eggs from the "Easter bunny" and coloring hard-boiled eggs at Easter. But, there is much more to the story of the Easter egg.

In very early times, the egg was honored during many rites-of-spring celebrations. The egg was a symbol of the universe and of nature's rebirth. Christians began to think of the egg as a symbol of the Resurrection. Also, as eggs were often given up as a lenten penance, Easter brought a return of the time when Christians could again eat eggs.

In Poland, many legends and lore about the egg arose. One Polish legend says that Mary, the Mother of Jesus, gave eggs to the soldiers at the foot of the cross asking them to be less cruel to her son. It is said that her tears fell on the eggs and the plain white shells became spotted with tears of bright colors.

Another story holds that when Mary Magdalene went to the tomb of Jesus to anoint his body she carried a basket of eggs with her. When she stopped at the tomb, she uncovered the eggs and discovered that the basket of white eggs had become a basket of rainbow colored ones.

During the Middle Ages people in many countries began coloring and decorating eggs for Easter. In 1290 it is believed that Edward I gave 450 gold-leafed and colored eggs as Easter gifts. In 1883, Alexander, the Russian Czar, had a goldsmith, Peter Faberge, make a special Easter gift for his wife, the Empress Marie—a golden egg.

Today we color eggs at Easter and remember the early Christians who looked for everyday items that could be used as symbols of Jesus' triumph over death. The Easter egg is a symbol of rebirth and a wonderful reminder of the salvation won for us by Jesus. (Craft directions on reverse.)

The Easter Egg

Special Materials Needed:

* an egg
* tissue paper (various shades)
* white glue with water (two parts glue/one part water)
* paintbrush
* yarn
* a small star sticker
* bobby pin or large needle
* glitter
* jar lid

Directions:

1. Chip a small hole in both ends of an egg and blow out the contents.
2. String a piece of yarn through both ends to make the egg hang. (Use a bobby pin or large sized sewing needle to thread.)
3. Place the star sticker at the bottom hole to keep the yarn from pulling back through.
4. Tear brightly colored tissue paper into very small pieces.
5. Spread the egg with the white glue mixture, small sections at a time. (Rest the egg in a jar lid while working so that the egg stays in place.)
6. Place torn tissue pieces on the area and brush with more glue mixture on top of the tissue.
7. Sprinkle the egg lightly with glitter while it is still damp or apply white glue and glitter after the tissue is dry.

Additional Activity:

* Hang the egg from a branch to make an "egg tree."

Christmas and Easter Holly

When we see dark, rich holly we think of Christmas, but originally holly was used during a festival to honor the Roman god Saturn. The ancient Romans decorated their homes with holly and gave holly wreaths as presents during their celebrations. Centuries later, Christians began celebrating the birth of Jesus during the same month of December. To avoid persecution from the Romans and still be able to decorate, Christians began decking their homes in holly too. As the Christian population increased, the custom of decorating homes with holly continued. After a time, holly lost its pagan roots and became a Christian symbol of Christmas.

The sharp points of the holly leaves also remind us of Jesus' crown of thorns and the red berries remind us of the blood Jesus shed for us. There is even a legend that the berries were originally white. When a gift of holly was presented to the Christ Child he pricked his finger on the leaf and a drop of blood touched the berries turning them red, foretelling his crucifixion. The evergreen of the leaf color stands for the Resurrection and eternal life.

Holly is a symbol of peace and joy, and certainly now intimately connected with the Christmas season, though it can serve as an apt reminder of Easter too.

Special Materials Needed:
- dark green, light green, and red construction paper
- hole punch

Directions:
1. Cut the leaf rectangle on the dark lines.
2. Fold the leaf on the dotted line.
3. Stack two or three small rectangles of green paper that are the same size as the pattern.
4. Fold all in half horizontally.
5. Fold the leaf pattern and place it over the stacked rectangles.
6. Cut along the outside line.
   (For younger children, trace the pattern.)
7. Open.
8. Glue the ends of several green leaves together.
9. Hole punch red dots. Glue to the leaf as desired.

Additional Activity:
- Place the completed projects as a border around the ceiling of the classroom.

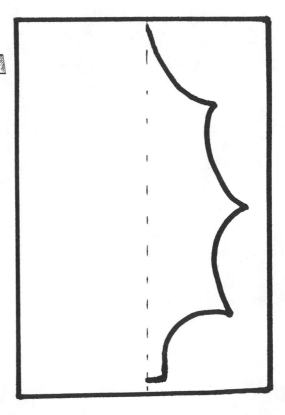

St. Patrick's Shamrock

Today when we see a shamrock it reminds us of St. Patrick and Ireland.

The shamrock held a special significance to the early Celtic clans of Ireland. The shamrock was a lucky emblem based on the Celtic sun wheel. When St. Patrick came to Ireland to convert the Druid people to Christianity he was met with opposition. He was challenged by a powerful Druid chieftain to explain the idea of the Holy Trinity. How could there be three persons in one God? St. Patrick thought for a moment and then reached to the ground and plucked a shamrock. As he held it up to the chief he pointed to its three leaves growing from one stem. The Celtic chief saw the relationship between this new doctrine and the lucky symbol. Not only was St. Patrick able to teach about Christianity to the masses, but the chieftain himself was converted.

Special Materials Needed:
- green and purple construction paper
- single hole punch

Directions:
1. Cut three identical hearts from green construction paper.
2. Glue all three hearts so that the tips are touching to form a shamrock.
3. Make a stem with scraps.
4. Form flowers by placing five purple hole punch dots in a circle. Scatter flowers over the shamrock plant.

Additional Activity:
- Make a green gelatin shamrock. Follow the directions for jigglers on the back of the box. Make sure to use about half the water called for in a regular gelatin recipe. When the green gelatin is set, cut three heart shapes for each shamrock (one heart for each person). Place the hearts so that the tips are touching to form a shamrock. Make a stem from left over gelatin. Tell the story of the shamrock. Eat the shamrock!

Christians and the Dogwood Tree

The dogwood tree is a small, gnarled tree. Its twisted, crooked limbs cannot be used for furniture or anything to be built with long, flat pieces of wood.

Legend says that the dogwood tree was once a large, towering tree. But, it was a dogwood tree that was cut down and used to make the cross on which Jesus suffered and died, according to the story.

The tree was sad that it was used in this manner. It hung its head low. God looked down on the tree and understood its sadness. He took pity on the tree and commanded that the dogwood tree would from then on grow as a small, twisted tree so that a cross could never again be fashioned from its wood. Then, the Lord blessed the flowers of the dogwood. The flower's four white or pink petals look like a cross and the tips of the petals are touched with a drop of red, like the blood Jesus shed for us. The yellow center resembles a tiny crown of thorns.

While we know that a tree can't be "sad," when we look at the dogwood and see the distinct flowers it's easy to see how the early Christians came to associate the tree with the crucifixion.

Special Materials Needed:
- light blue construction paper
- brown or black paint
- white or pink paint
- red paint
- green paint
- a straw
- paintbrush

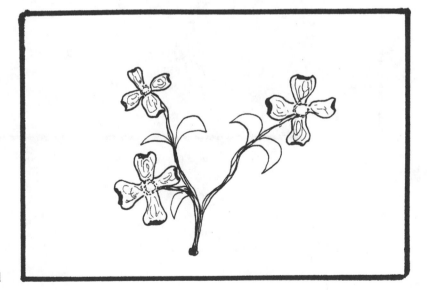

Directions:
1. On a light blue piece of construction paper, place a dark brown or black dot of paint.
2. With a straw, blow the dot upward on the paper. As it runs along the paper, it will look like a limb.
3. Place a yellow dot of paint on the paper as the center of the flower.
4. With white (or pink) paint, make four thumbprints from the yellow center.
5. Before the white (or pink) paint is dry, use a fine brush to put a tiny drip of red paint at the ends of each thumbprint petal.
6. Add a few green leaves on the dogwood limb if desired.

Mary's Gold

The marigold is a sturdy flower, bright and sunny. The yellow, orange, and red blossoms smile brightly in the sun. The flower is associated with the lion, an animal of legend known for its brave heart and courage. It is an herb of the sun. Early Christians placed the flowers around statues of the Blessed Mother offering the blossoms in place of coins. Marigold became known as "Mary's gold."

Legend says that Mary used the blossoms as coins. During the flight into Egypt the Holy Family was stopped by a band of thieves. They took Mary's purse, but when they opened it, marigolds fell out.

Marigold blooms represent the golden rays of glory that are often shown around the Blessed Lady's head. The flower is used in celebrating most of the chief Marian feast days.

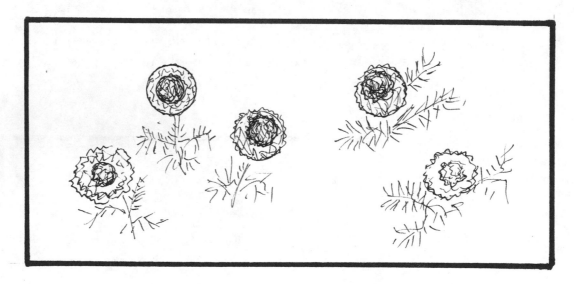

Special Materials Needed:
- yellow, orange, red, and green paint
- a coarse sponge cut into various sizes of small circles
- lids for paint
- paintbrush or craft stick
- white or manila construction paper

Directions:
1. Pour yellow, orange, and red paint in separate lids.
2. Dip sponges in paint. Tap paint on the paper starting with the largest sponge circle; overlap colors as desired. (Allow coats to dry between applications.)
3. When the blossoms are dry, paint in stems and leaves with a brush or craft stick.

The Legend of St. Valentine

Legend holds that Valentine's Day on February 14 is named in memory of St. Valentine of Rome. Little is know about him, but what *is* known is fascinating.

St. Valentine of Rome was born in the third century. It is believed that he gave children flowers from his garden. St. Valentine angered Emperor Claudius because he had helped Christian martyrs. When he was imprisoned the children missed him and threw bouquets through the prison bars. While in prison Valentine fell in love with the jailer's daughter. He cured her blindness and wrote love letters to her. He signed his last letter "From Your Valentine." Nevertheless, the Emperor had Valentine beheaded on February 14. Two hundred years later Pope Gelasius set February 14 as a day to honor the saint.

When Christianity became more widespread, the pagan fertility festival of Lupercalia was changed to honor St. Valentine who became the patron saint of lovers. Another story of Valentine says that at his death in 269 a pink almond tree near his grave burst into bloom as a symbol of everlasting love.

Special Materials Needed:
- pink tissue paper, cut in 1 1/2" squares
- 4" square of red construction paper
- green paint or markers
- white or manila construction paper
- pencil with an eraser

Directions:
1. On the white or manila construction paper paint some Almond Tree limbs. With green paint or markers start at one point at the bottom of the paper and moving upward make some limbs and some small curled leaves.
2. Put a pink tissue paper square onto the eraser part of the pencil.
3. Put a dot of glue on the paper and affix the tissue piece to the stem.
4. Repeat with other pink squares until you've made as many Almond "blossoms" as desired.
5. Fold the red square in half. Trace a wide C with a pointed bottom. Hold the fold while you cut the C. Open to reveal a heart shape.
6. Glue the red heart to the bottom of the stem like a "vase."

The Passion Vine

The Passion Vine is a beautiful, distinct, climbing plant. Its leaves and flowers are quite unique. It isn't a surprise, therefore, that legend has grown up around this vine. Each part of the plant—flower, leaves, and vine—plays a role in the legend.

One thing surprising about this legend is the fact that there is specific historical documentation of the time and place of origin. The first mention of the symbolism was by a Mexican Augustinian friar, Emmanuel de Villegas, reporting it, with sketches, in Europe in 1610. Later, Passion Flowers were preserved in wax and sold in gift shops with a card attached detailing the symbolism to Our Lord's Crucifixion. The legend continued and spread.

Passion Vine grows in my garden. It is one plant that attracts and feeds the Gulf Flitterary butterfly caterpillar. It's nice to think that the plant that symbolizes the crucifixion feeds and nurtures the caterpillar that will turn into a beautiful butterfly—a symbol of the Resurrection.

Directions:
1. Copy or reproduce the Passion Vine.
2. Color the picture in purples, green, and red where "blood" is denoted.

Additional Activities:
- If available, bring in a Passion Vine plant or flower for examination.
- Make a Resurrection Butterfly (see page 125) to go along with the Passion Vine craft.

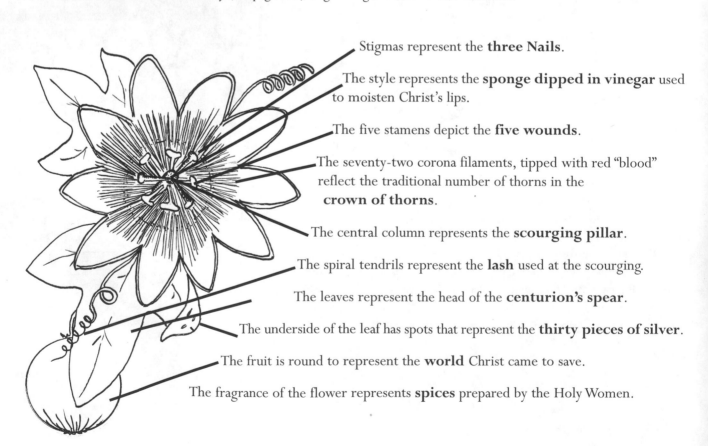

Stigmas represent the **three Nails**.

The style represents the **sponge dipped in vinegar** used to moisten Christ's lips.

The five stamens depict the **five wounds**.

The seventy-two corona filaments, tipped with red "blood" reflect the traditional number of thorns in the **crown of thorns**.

The central column represents the **scourging pillar**.

The spiral tendrils represent the **lash** used at the scourging.

The leaves represent the head of the **centurion's spear**.

The underside of the leaf has spots that represent the **thirty pieces of silver**.

The fruit is round to represent the **world** Christ came to save.

The fragrance of the flower represents **spices** prepared by the Holy Women.

5

Holy Days and
Church Seasons

Our lives ebb and flow with a variety of seasons; from the natural seasons of fall, winter, spring, and summer to the seasons of our own personal experience: lows and highs, gloom and exhilaration, suffering and rebirth.

The Church Year is also divided into seasons that mark our spiritual journey, both individually and collectively.

Advent begins the Church Year. This is a time of joyful anticipation for Jesus' second coming and for his entrance into the world as a newborn baby on Christmas Day. Christmas is a second Church season, culminating with the Feast of the Epiphany, the visit of the Wise Men.

Lent means "springtime." It is a forty-day season of penance in preparation for Easter. The Easter season extends from Easter Sunday to Pentecost, a time of fifty days.

The rest of the Church Year is called Ordinary Time, though throughout all the seasons many special or holy days commemorating saints and other significant times in the lives of Jesus and Mary are marked and celebrated.

The activities and projects in this chapter are randomly arranged with the expectation that they can be used whenever the season or lesson theme is deemed appropriate.

Egg Carton Advent Calendar

Advent is a season of waiting.

Waiting is not easy. Often when we are told we have to wait for something it makes us frustrated. We want to find a way to make the time go faster. We want to speed up the process and help it along. Still, we know that if we wait for something the anticipation makes the reward that much greater. Anyone who has ever waited for a new baby to be born knows that the reward is very much worth it.

Advent calendars have been used for many years to show the number of days of waiting. They help us "count down" to the blessed event.

This calendar uses common items and recycles old greeting cards from past years to create a new way to help us prepare for the coming of Christ.

Special Materials Needed:
- two egg cartons
- 8 1/2" x 11" poster board
- marker
- wrapped, hard candy
- old Christmas cards or colorful scraps of Christmas wrapping paper. (If these are unavailable, the children may draw in items as needed.)

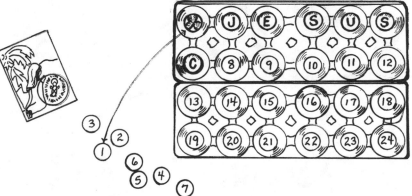

Directions:
1. Copy and glue the JESUS CHRIST IS BORN! message page 92 to heavy poster board.
2. Cut pictures out of old Christmas cards and paste them over the empty circle sections of the message. (Do not cover the JESUS CHRIST IS BORN! message.) Color and decorate as desired.
3. Cut the lids off of two egg cartons.
4. Number the bottom of all the egg cups from 1 to 24.
5. Cut half way under each number so that each egg cup numbered piece can be torn off in turn.
6. Place a piece of candy on each circle of the message page (optional).
7. Turn the egg cup sections upside down to cover the message and candy. Glue both bottoms in place over the "Jesus Christ is born" message.
8. Place a book or similar weight on top and allow the Advent Calendar to dry.
9. Open a number cup each day beginning with December 1.

Additional Activity:
- Pair up the children so that each has a "secret Santa." Encourage the children to do a good deed (preferably in secret) for their partner each day of Advent.

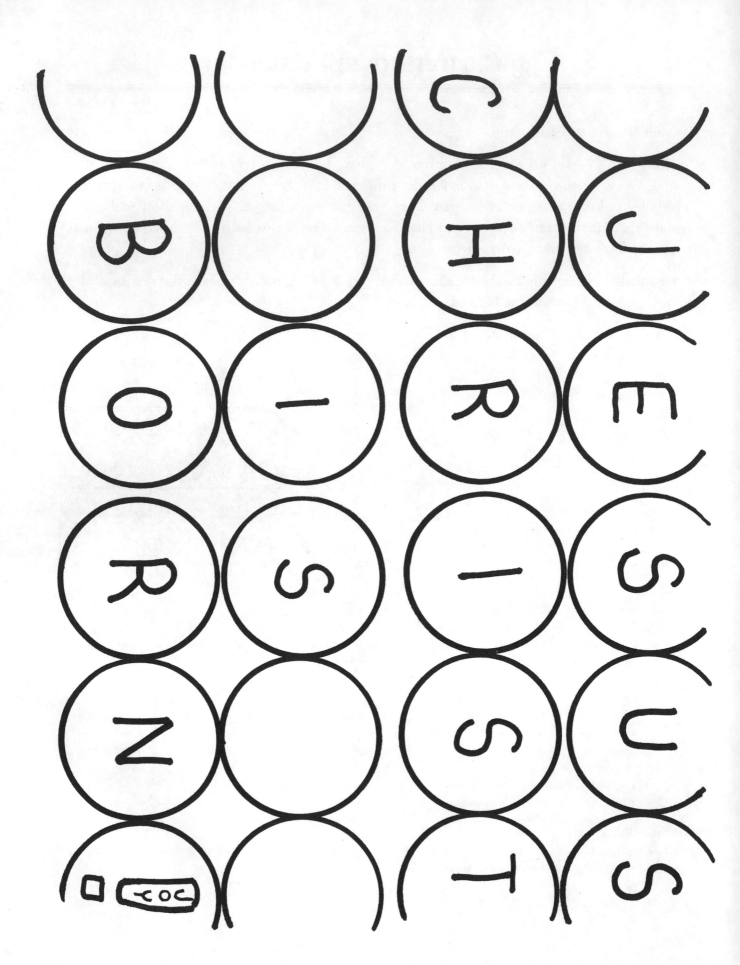

Miniature Advent Wreath

The four candles of an Advent wreath mark the four weeks of Advent and remind us that Christ is the light of the world. Three of the candles are purple, reflecting the liturgical colors of the season. The candle for the third week of Advent is pink or rose, noting the impending joyful anticipation of the coming of Christ.

By making their own miniature wreath, children can take the Advent Wreath with them into their own rooms or to some other place in the home. (Directions are below.)

Special Note: It is not advisable for the children to light the candles. Instead, the children should be given four small squares of gold paper that can be twisted around the wick to simulate a burning candle. (Tape the four small squares of gold paper or ribbon "flames" under the cups to be used as needed.)

Special Materials Needed:

- green construction paper
- white glue
- green tissue paper
- a four cup section of an egg carton bottom
- three purple, birthday cake candles
- one pink or rose birthday cake candle
- four small squares of gold paper or ribbon
- red hole punch dots, glitter, ribbon, purchased mini ribbon roses or miniature lilies (optional; see page 94)

Directions:
1. Place the four-section egg carton upside-down.
2. Push a candle through the center of each cup.
3. Glue small pieces of green paper and tissue to the entire cup.
4. Decorate with red "berry" hole punch dots, ribbon, mini roses, lilies or glitter as desired.
5. Twist a piece of gold paper or ribbon around each wick on the first Sunday of each week.

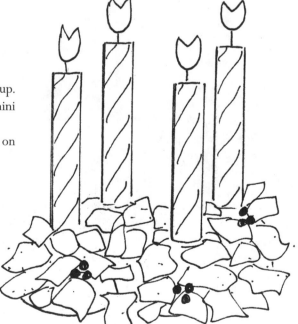

Miniature Lilies

The lily is a special symbol of the Easter season but it is also a sign of the purity of Christ's birth. The lily and the rose (a symbol of Mary) are often used to adorn altars and tables during various seasons. It is nice to have additional ways to present the lily so that it can be used on cards, as small gifts, or even twined around a pipe cleaner or baggie tie to make a lovely napkin ring or a decoration for a mini Advent Wreath (see page 93). Also, several miniature lilies can be tied together with a bow to make a lapel pin.

Have the children suggest other ways to use the miniature lilies.

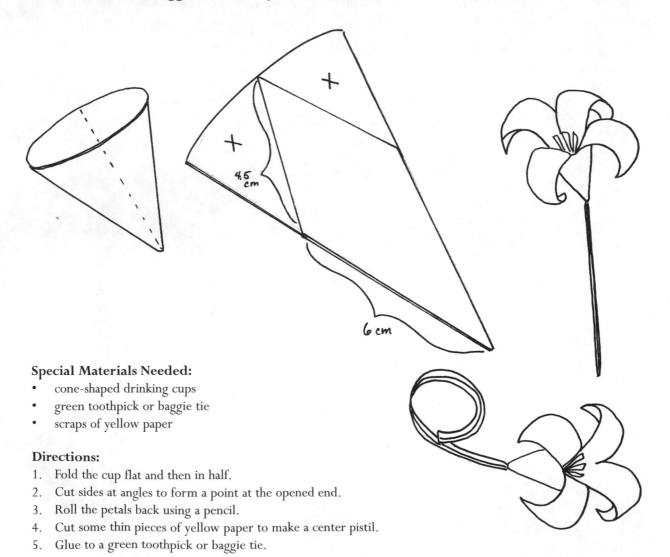

Special Materials Needed:
•   cone-shaped drinking cups
•   green toothpick or baggie tie
•   scraps of yellow paper

Directions:
1. Fold the cup flat and then in half.
2. Cut sides at angles to form a point at the opened end.
3. Roll the petals back using a pencil.
4. Cut some thin pieces of yellow paper to make a center pistil.
5. Glue to a green toothpick or baggie tie.

Additional Activities:
•   Use the lily for a napkin ring. (Wrap the baggie tie into a circle.)
•   Place several lilies with leaves (green paper scraps) in a miniature clay pot. (Put a wad of clay in the bottom of the pot to hold the stems.) Cover the stem with moss or mini pebbles.

The Nativity

It is important that children understand the true beauty and magical nature of Christmas stems from a solemn, single birth. The crèche is a quiet scene of a humble birth in a stable. This crèche is one that children can make and hold in their hands, helping to bring the true magic of the season home. (Directions on reverse.)

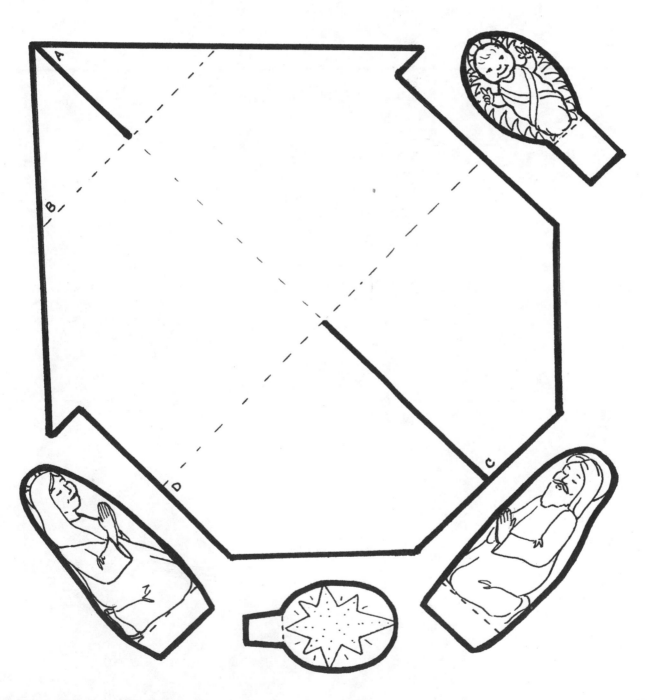

The Nativity

Directions:
1. Color all the pieces.
2. Cut out all the pieces on the dark lines.
3. Fold all the pieces inward on the dotted lines.
4. Overlap and glue A to B, and C to D to form the stable.
5. Glue Jesus, Mary, Joseph, and the star in place.

Additional Activities:
- The crèche may be made smaller or enlarged.
- You may wish to provide only the stable piece and allow the children to draw a small Jesus, Mary, and Joseph to put in the crèche. Provide small sticker stars to place on the rooftop.

Epiphany

An epiphany is "a sudden realization of the meaning of something." In the case of the feast of the Epiphany, the three magi realized that the baby in their presence was God. Tradition tells us that the Magi were: Melchior with the gift of gold, Balthasar with the gift of frankincense, and Caspar with the gift of myrrh.

When I was a little girl, my mother put up the Christmas tree just a few days prior to Christmas. When she unwrapped the magi from the nativity set, she placed them at the far end of the room. Each day after Christmas she would move the magi closer to the stable that sat under the tree. I watched as the magi advanced across the top of the television, across the bookcase, behind an overstuffed chair and finally on the morning of the Epiphany they arrived at the crèche. She placed them lovingly in front of the crib.

We never took down our tree until the magi's visit. Mother reminded us that the Epiphany was a very special time since it marked the spreading of the good news to all people. The three wise men traversing across our living room will always be a vivid Christmas memory for me. (Directions on next page.)

Epiphany

Special Materials Needed:
* empty paper towel or bathroom tissue tube

Directions:
1. Color the magi.
2. Cut the magi out on the dark lines.
3. Cut the tube into three 1" sections.
4. Glue the bases of the magi puppets to the tube sections.

Additional Activity:
* Sing, "We Three Kings," as the children march their puppets around the room.

Lenten Boxes

Lent is a time of sacrifice, reflection, and prayer. A lenten box is a traditional place for the children to keep coins collected through their personal sacrifices. The collected coins can be used as an offering for the poor. (Directions on the reverse.)

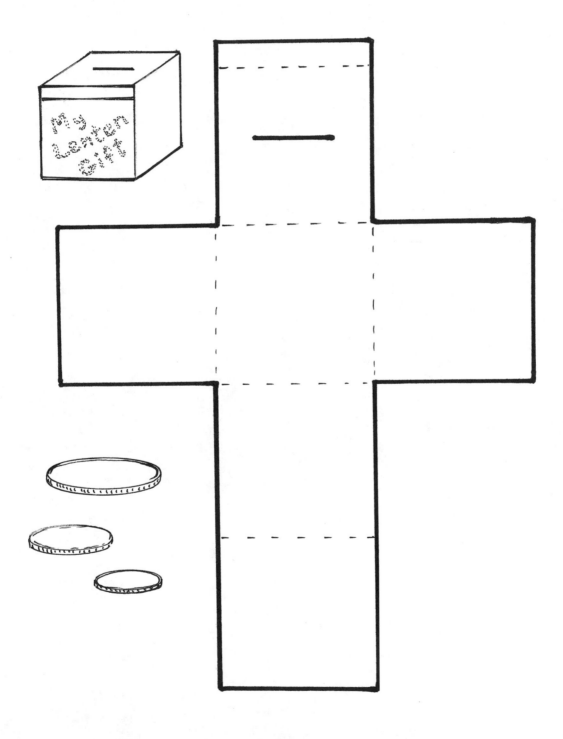

Lenten Boxes

Special Materials Needed:
- violet or purple poster board
- glitter or glitter markers

Directions:
1. Trace the pattern onto a violet or purple piece of poster board. Deeply pencil in the dotted lines.
2. Cut out the pattern.
3. Fold on the dotted lines to make a box.
4. Make a money slit on one square.
5. Form the box; tape its sides and top.
6. Decorate with glitter markers.

Additional Activities:
- Have the children use any small box with a lid and cover it with purple paint or paper. They can also decorate with glitter.
- Remind children to give up small treats and put the money saved in the box for missions.
- Collect the change on or prior to Easter and send the money to missions via your church.

The Easter lily is a symbol of the Lord's Resurrection. The lily represents the purity and hope of the resurrection. It is a white flower that blooms in glory during the Easter season. Altars are festooned with the beautiful, magnificent blooms. (Directions on reverse.)

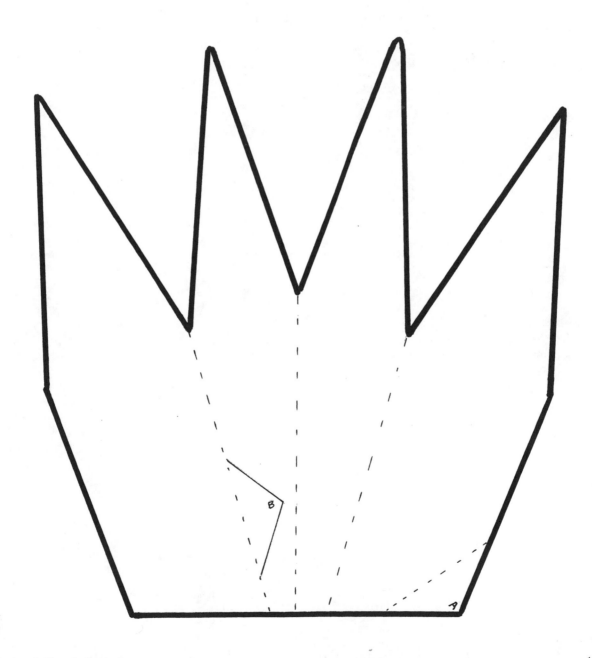

The Easter Lily

Special Materials:
- yellow paper
- green pipe cleaner or green straw
- green paper (optional)

Directions:
1. Cut out the lily on the bold dark lines.
2. Fold on the dotted lines.
3. Roll the lily so that A touches B at the thin black line.
4. Glue A on top of B.
5. Roll each lily petal down using a pencil.
6. Cut a few 6" x 1/2" strips of yellow paper.
7. Glue the tips of the strips down into the center of the lily.
8. Fold up the bottom of the lily and staple or glue in place.
9. Glue or staple the lily to a green pipe cleaner or green straw.
10. Make leaves, if desired, for the stem. Slightly roll green paper around a pencil. Glue the leaves to the stem.

Additional Activities:
- Have each child make a flower and then place the flowers in a vase on the Prayer Table at Easter time.
- Use several lilies on a bulletin board to bring attention to a special message (e. g., "The Lord is Risen!").
- Push the bottom of the lily stem down into a clump of soft modeling clay. Then, put the clump into the bottom of a small clay plot. Fill the pot with moss or Easter straw.

Pentecost

Pentecost was originally a Jewish festival to celebrate the first harvest of spring. On the Pentecost after Jesus' resurrection and ascension, it was the day that the Holy Spirit came to the apostles who were gathered in the Upper Room where they had shared the Last Supper with Jesus. The word Pentecost means "fiftieth day" as it fell fifty days after Passover.

The Holy Spirit came to the apostles as in "tongues of fire." Another symbol of the Holy Spirit is a dove. Both of these symbols are represented in this activity. (Directions on page 104.)

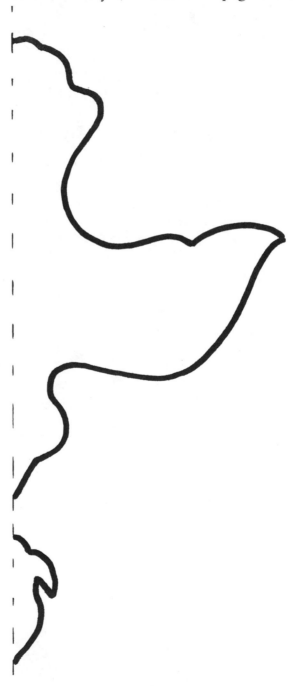

Pentecost

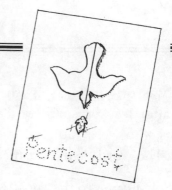

Special Materials Needed:
- construction paper (two contrasting colors)
- glitter (optional)

Directions:
1. Fold the dove and flame on the dotted center line.
2. Hold the fold, and cut out the dove and flame on the dark lines.
3. Glitter the flame, if desired.
4. Place small dots of glue on the back of the fold line of the dove and flame and glue them in a 3-D effect to a contrasting color of construction paper.

Trinity Sunday

The Trinity is the basic tenet of our faith. We celebrate God the Father, the Son, and the Holy Spirit; three persons in one God. Trinity Sunday is celebrated after Pentecost Sunday.

Several symbols and teaching tools have been used to help us better understand the Trinity. The shamrock is one of the symbols used to explain the Trinity. The shamrock is one leaf with three parts. Many years ago when the Trinity was introduced to me three long tapered candles were used. One was placed in a holder and the other two were lighted. As the third one was lighted, all three flames were held together. Three distinct candles and three distinct flames, but all three flames burned as one. It was impossible to distinguish the individuality of the three flames and yet each candlewick was distinct with its own flame.

This project offers another way for the students to understand the Trinity. (Directions on the reverse.)

Trinity Sunday

Special Materials Needed:
*   colored construction paper

Directions:
1. Cut out the triangle (inside and out) on the dark lines and glue it to the center of a piece of contrasting colored paper.
2. Color and cut out the symbols for God the Father (crown), God the Son (cross), and God the Holy Spirit (dove).
3. Glue the pieces onto the triangle, one on each point.

Additional Activities:
*   Show the children the three-candle concept of explaining the Trinity.
*   Discuss the concept of how one person has many roles: mother/father, husband/wife, sister/brother, son/daughter, doctor, teacher, nurse, electrician, etc. One person can be many "people." (This concept isn't the same as three persons in the Trinity, of course, but is at least understandable to children.)

6

More Faith Sharing

The religious education of children is an interesting endeavor because it can be accomplished in so many different kinds of settings and at so many different times.

For example, in a family setting, children learn from their parents and their siblings. Older brothers and sisters love to serve as examples and helpers for younger family members. These activities incorporate a variety of lessons and themes and can be used in a home or classroom setting. They can be done both individually and in groups.

Remind the children that when "two or more" are gathered in Jesus' name, he is there with them. Working through these activities is a form of faith sharing and prayer.

Bible Verse Mobile

The Bible is a source of divine revelation and inspiration. Even young children can learn about God and be inspired by him through the reading of Bible verses. Some parts are obviously designed to help us praise God.

Provide some of the simplest and prettiest Bible verses. For example: "I love you, God, my strength" (Psalm 18). "God is my shepherd, I lack nothing" (Psalm 24). Peruse the book of Psalms to find many other verses to serve as inspiration to your children.

Special Materials Needed:
*   three 3" x 5" cards per child
*   yarn

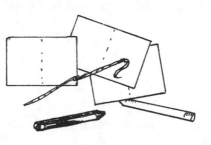

Directions:
1. Fold the 3" x 5" cards in half.
2. Choose a Bible verse, prayer, or commandment. Print the verse on the first card.
3. On the second card, draw a picture to illustrate the words on the first card.
4. On the third card, write an application verse; i.e., what the verse means.
    For example:
    Card 1: "God is my shepherd, I lack nothing."
    Card 2: Picture of Jesus, Good Shepherd, Lamb, etc.
    Card 3: "God always takes care of us."
5. Glue the cards to each other with a piece of yarn laced through the center.

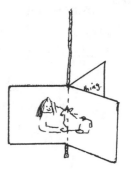

Additional Activities:
*   For a group activity, divide the children into groups of three. Have each child work on one card.
*   Display the mobiles by hanging them in the classroom.

Rose Window Puzzle

Our parish community is our family of faith. Many parishes have a logo that represents their community. Or, perhaps your church has a stained-glass window, grotto area, or altarpiece that is very identifiable. The moment people see it, they know that it represents your specific church. It may even be depicted on your church bulletin or letterhead.

Our parish church has a very beautiful rose window of the Holy Spirit. I have heard little ones call it "the bird window." If you don't have, or are unable to obtain a representation of your specific church, you may wish to enlarge and use this picture. (Directions on reverse.)

Rose Window Puzzle

Directions:

1. Cut out or copy the rose window page. Enlarge if possible.
2. Cut the side "pie" pieces out on the dark lines.
3. Color the pieces.
4. Place the Holy Spirit circle at the center of a piece of paper.
5. Glue the pieces in place to complete the window.
   While doing so the children should tell something special about themselves and their church.

Additional Activity:

- Copy your parish's logo or representative symbol and have it enlarged. Then, carefully cut the logo into puzzle pieces. Give a piece to each child. Have the children tell something special about themselves and work to put the puzzle pieces in place. After every child has had a turn remind the children that their parish is not complete without each and every person. Say, "Together we make a whole, a complete and loving family of God."
- Place your fingers over one of the pieces. Show how the window and parish is not complete unless we all work together to make it whole.

Flowers of Faith

Our church community is made up of many people who come together to share their talents. Many of these talents are utilized at liturgy. Some people help in a way that we can see, but many people also work "behind the scenes." Some people have a special talent for singing or playing a musical instrument, some people are lectors (readers), and some people prepare the church altar. Some people decorate the church for the different seasons. Some people greet us; some seat us. Children help as altar servers and often bring the gifts to the altar. Other church members come together to clean the church and the church grounds.

Think about and discuss the many opportunities for helping in and around the church. Remind the children that the church is theirs and that they should be already thinking of what gifts they might bring to the church some day. (Directions on reverse.)

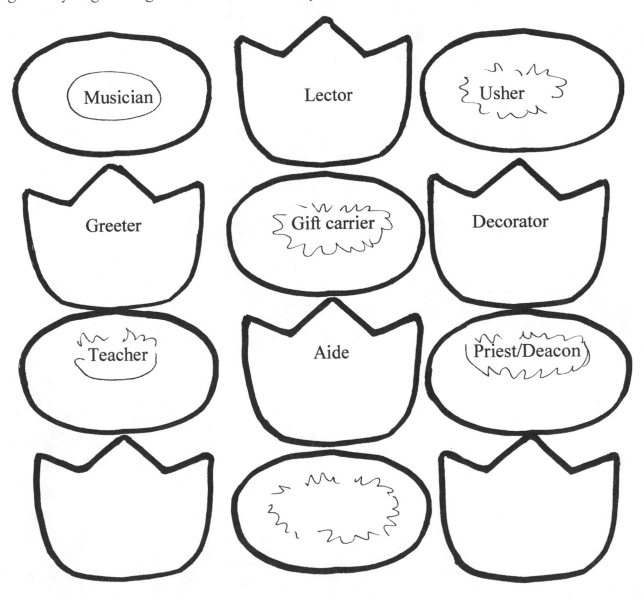

Flowers of Faith

Special Materials Needed:

- envelopes
- straws or craft sticks

Directions:

1. Cut out the flowers.
2. Glue or tape each to a straw or craft stick.
3. To make a flower pot, glue a business envelope closed; cut it in half.
4. Cut the open sides 1/2" at each seam and fold them down.
5. Fold the bottom sides back slightly.
6. Print your name on the outside of the pot.
7. Put one, two, three or more flowers in the pot to show what helping jobs you do at church now, or would like to do when you get a little older.
8. Tape the flowers in the pot, if desired.

Upon This Rock

When Jesus changed Simon's name to Peter, meaning "Rock," he said, "Upon this rock, I will build my church."

We are all called on to be "rocks" or strong building blocks of our church. Just as Peter was to lead the disciples and send them out to spread Jesus' word, we too are called upon to take the strength of our faith out to others. We are to share our love for Jesus and his message. We build on the rock, going forward in faith.

A strong visual will make this concept more real and make a greater impression than just telling about something.

Special Materials Needed:
- one large rock for the class
- one length of yarn for each child (6' to 10')

Directions:
1. While the teacher holds the rock, tie the end of the 6' to 10' lengths of yarn to it.
2. Hold the end of a piece of yarn and slowly walk out away from the rock to remind you that you should take the good news of Christ, the foundation of the church, out into the world.

Additional Activity:
- Have the children help identify all the ways that God is sending us out to spread the love of the church.

Attendance Incentive Headband/Streamer

Help the children to know the imperative nature of attending religious education class on a consistent basis. There are many loving, subtle ways to encourage and nurture this responsibility.

The first day children come to class they should be given a small treat and be reminded that they are important and their attendance is a wonderful, positive step in learning about the Lord and his love for us. They should know that each class builds on their faith and makes them stronger disciples of the Lord.

An attendance chart that records their presence serves as a visual motivator and rewards their commitment. Tell the children that their attendance strip will be cut out and used as a band to "crown" their attendance on the last day of class. (Older children that may not want to wear crowns can make an attendance banner or streamer.)

Directions for Catechist:

1. On a large piece of poster board grid out a long thin attendance strip representing each child's name. Make sure the squares that represent the dates of attendance are large enough to accommodate a sticker or decorative stamp.
2. On the first day of class, show and explain the attendance chart and give each child a sticker to put in the first dated column.
3. Each class thereafter give each child in attendance a sticker, star, or allow them to stamp the appropriate box.
4. On the last day of class, cut the long strip for each child. Do one of the following: A) Make a crown. Form the strip into a headband; B) Make a streamer. Attach the strip to a dowel rod; or C) Make a banner.

Apostle Word Find

The twelve apostles were from many walks of life. They were common people called on by Jesus to do uncommon things. The word apostle means "one sent."

The apostles are named in: Matthew 10:2-4, Mark 3:13-19, Luke 6:12-16, and Acts 1:13-14. Read one of these scripture accounts of their call by Jesus.

Directions:
1. Find and circle the names of the apostles.
2. Answer the questions that follow.

The Twelve Apostles

Peter, Andrew, James son of Zebedee, John, Philip, Bartholomew, Thomas, Matthew, James son of Alphaeus, Thaddaeus, Simon the Zealot, Judas.

Questions:
1. This disciple's name had been Simon, but was changed by Jesus to a name that means "rock." His name is _____.
2. Name two sets of brothers who were disciples:
    _____ and _____
    _____ and _____

T	W	E	L	V	E	X	D	I	S	C	I	P	L	E	S	L
X	P	E	T	E	R	A	R	O	C	K	X	N	O	R	D	S
B	R	O	A	N	D	R	E	W	N	T	S	R	M	J	K	R
J	O	H	N	L	O	P	E	D	S	R	Y	Z	U	X	M	N
A	X	B	A	R	T	H	O	L	O	M	E	W	B	D	F	O
M	G	J	P	H	I	L	I	P	L	K	I	Q	S	R	Y	P
E	T	H	O	M	A	S	P	M	A	T	T	H	E	W	Z	Q
S	H	J	A	M	E	S	O	F	A	L	P	H	A	E	U	S
O	Q	M	B	O	N	S	I	M	O	N	Z	E	A	L	O	T
F	S	R	T	H	A	D	D	A	E	U	S	W	G	X	H	J
Z	A	T	C	T	D	E	U	F	V	J	U	D	A	S	K	U

(Solution on p.128)

Apostle Word Find

Additional Activity:

- Create your own "Disciples of Today" word find using all the names of the students in your class or names of the people in your family or any other combination you prefer. On graph paper or on the grid below, fill in the names you chose to put in your word find. Copy the names on a separate answer key. Then fill in all of the blank spaces with random letters. (Use all upper case letters.) Trade your word find with a friend. Give them the list of names they need to find.

Disciples of Today

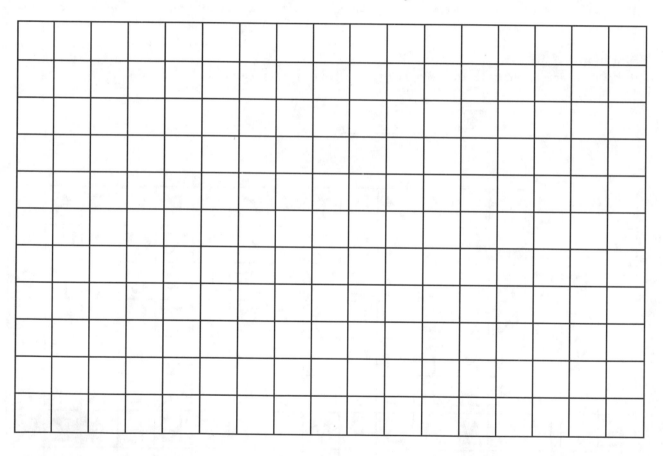

Blessing of the Pets

October 4 is the feast day of St. Francis of Assisi. St. Francis is known for his love for all of creation. He had a fellowship with all people, animals, and the rest of the natural world. He called the sun "brother" and the moon "sister." He was one with all of God's creations.

Francis' mission was clear: Help people find reconciliation
with themselves, others and God . . . stone by stone,
rebuilding individual lives, communities and the world.

Many things have been written about St. Francis of Assisi, and there are many famous stories of his love for animals. One story tells how Francis saw a flock of birds and walked toward them. Instead of flying away when he approached, they gathered around him and listened while he preached of God's love and care for them. Another famous story of St. Francis and animals tells of Francis in the village of Gubbio. A wolf had been terrorizing the people, killing many villagers. St. Francis bravely went out into the woods and found the beast. The beast bared its teeth, but Francis raised his arm and blessed the animal. Immediately the animal went to its knees. Francis asked the wolf to never kill again, the wolf agreed and soon it became a pet of the townspeople who lovingly fed and cared for it the rest of its days.

On or near October 4 we remember the love that Francis had for animals by blessing our own pets. (Directions on reverse.)

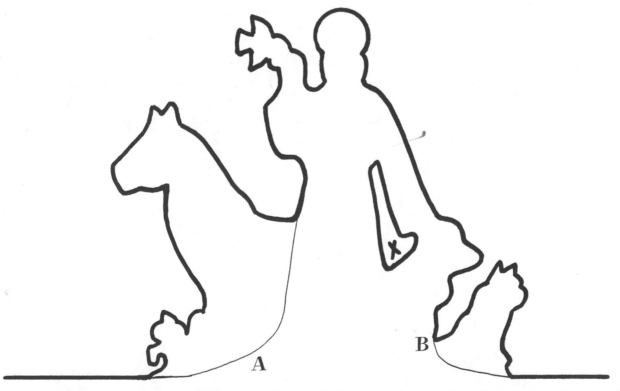

Please bless our pets, Oh Lord, and keep them in your loving care.

Blessing of the Pets

Special Materials Needed:
- dark construction paper
- white or manila construction paper
- magazine photos of animals

Directions:
1. Cut out the silhouette of St. Francis and the animals from page 117. Note that two different lines are shown. Older children or adults may wish to cut the entire silhouette (Francis, bird, dog, cat, horse and squirrel). Younger children may wish to use the easier cut lines A and B (Francis, bird, and dog).
2. Use the silhouette as a pattern to cut the silhouette again, this time from black or dark paper. (Place the pattern flush with a piece of dark paper, staple or paperclip the bottom in place, or for smaller children, lightly glue the pattern with rubber cement so that it can be removed after cutting.)
3. Glue the dark silhouette on a white or manila piece of paper.
4. Cut out pictures of animals from magazines. Make a collage of animals. Place the dark silhouette featuring St. Francis at the bottom of the collage.

Additional Activities:
- Find stories of St. Francis. Tell of his life and times and especially his love for all creatures.
- Find out if your parish has a blessing of the pets and obtain a copy of the blessing that is used. Share it with the children.
- For very young children a teacher or parent may wish to cut out the silhouette of the upper portion of St. Francis with the bird and dog only (lines A and B). Have the child paste the St. Francis silhouette to a colored piece of paper or a 3" x 5" index card to make a bookmark.
- Make a hatband hat for children to wear to a blessing of the pets celebration (see sketch above).

"He's Got the Whole World in His Hands" Spinner

Children love to sing. A craft to go along with a favorite song like, "He's Got the Whole World in His Hands" will make an impression on the child and the "magic" of a flip-picture will make singing the song even more fun. When talking about creation, this craft can help a child to visualize the concept that God holds us all in his loving hands. The movement created by the child as the picture spins back and forth involves visual and tactile stimuli, but mostly it's just plain fun! (Directions on back.)

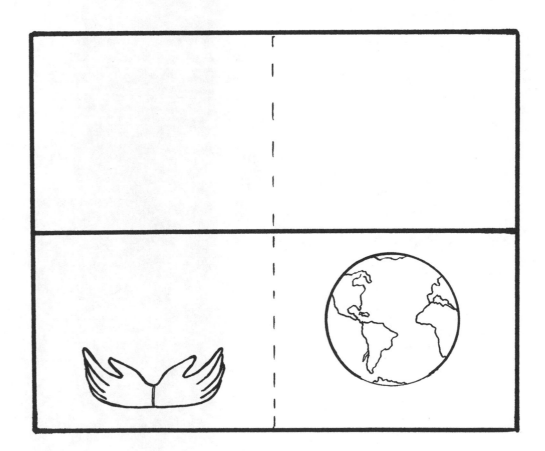

"He's Got the Whole World in His Hands" Spinner

Special Materials Needed:

- markers, crayons, or colored pencils
- a rounded toothpick

Fig.1 Fig. 2 Fig. 3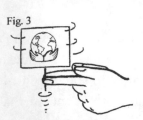

Directions:

1. Color the world and hands.
2. Cut out the rectangle on the bold outer line.
3. Carefully fold the bottom rectangle on the dotted center line with the pictures facing out (fig. 1).
4. Insert about half of a round toothpick into the fold.
5. Glue the rectangle shut with half of the toothpick inside (fig. 2).
6. When dry, place the bottom half of the toothpick between the index fingers of both hands and spin the picture back and forth (fig. 3). The hands will appear to be holding the world.

Additional Activities:

- Play the song, "He's Got the Whole World in His Hands" and sing along.
- Try having the children create a spinner of their own with the blank rectangle. *Hint*: Have them hold their first drawing up to the light to see where the second drawing needs to be placed so that the pictures work together.

Jesus the Carpenter

Jesus learned carpentry from St. Joseph. He likely spent most of his life on earth working at that trade.

A carpenter is a person who builds things and fixes things made of wood. A carpenter takes a plain piece of wood and fashions it into something unique. How wonderful to think that Jesus was a carpenter. We know that Jesus was sent from God to "build and mend lives." We can call Jesus the Master Builder. His love and guidance transforms us.

This activity employs many of the carpenter tools mentioned in the Bible (e.g., 1 Sm 13:19-20; Jgs 4:21; Is 10:15, 44:13) and tools known to be in existence during Greco-Roman times. (Directions are on the following page.)

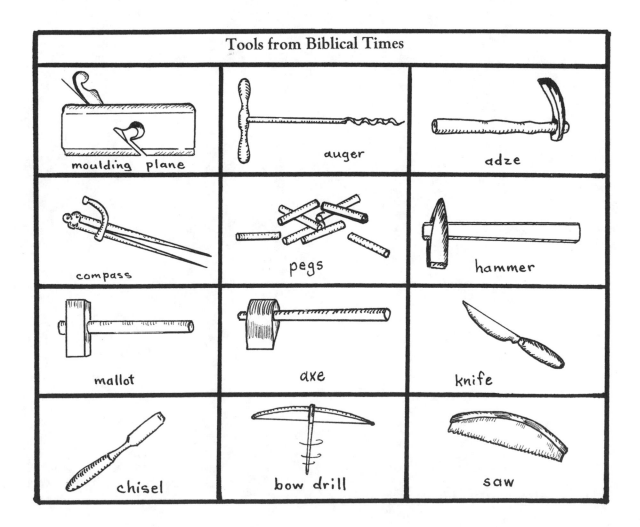

Tools from Biblical Times

moulding plane	auger	adze
compass	pegs	hammer
mallot	axe	knife
chisel	bow drill	saw

Jesus the Carpenter

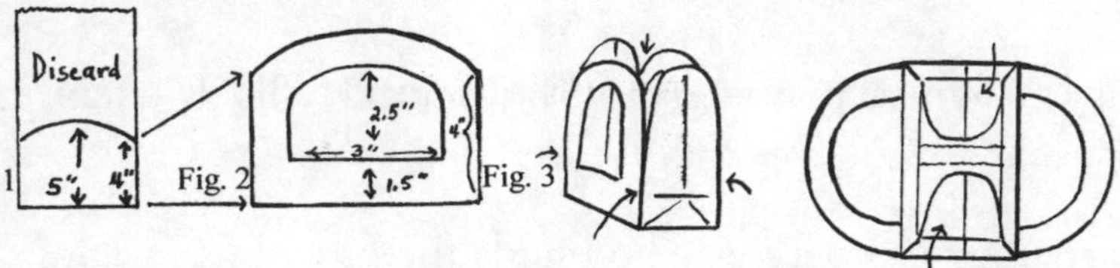

Special Materials Needed:
- brown lunch bag
- ruler

Fig. 1   Fig. 2   Fig. 3   Fig. 4

Directions:
1. With bag closed, cut the top arch. Discard top (fig. 1).
2. On both sides, trace the area to be cut out (fig. 2).
3. Cut out both side handle areas.
4. Cut the four corners down along creases to 1 1/2" from bottom (fig. 3).
5. Fold sides down and inside. Glue or tape, if desired (fig. 4).
6. Fold the handles up. Glue handles together at center only (fig. 5).
7. Color and cut out the tools from the previous page
   and put them in the box.

Fig. 5

Additional Activities:
- Children should be reminded that by our good example, our good works, our prayer and our financial support of the Church we are all called on to help build the kingdom of God.
- Sing or play a song that reinforces this concept while the children are working (e.g., "City of God").
- Discuss the purpose of the tools and show the correlation between Jesus being a builder with wood and a builder of God's kingdom.

"Thank You God" Nature Walk

There are so many wonderful things in nature for which we can be thankful. Nature's bounty is a special joy for children. Little children love to collect leaves, stones, and seeds. They love to walk in rain and snow, jump in puddles, and feel the warm sun on their faces. They love to feel sand pour through their fingers and mud squish between their toes.

A nature walk is always fun and can be an obvious occasion for giving thanks.

Special Materials Needed:
- poster board
- dark marker

Directions:
1. From poster board cut out the outline of several large leaf shapes. (Make a symmetrical leaf pattern by folding a piece of newspaper and cutting half a leaf shape. Open the pattern and trace it on the poster board.)
2. Print "Thank You God!" on each leaf.
3. Go on a nature walk and have the children collect fallen leaves. Glue these items to the poster board leaves to make collages.

Fishers of People

Many of the apostles were fishermen. Jesus told the first apostles that they would fish for people instead. We may think it sounds funny at first to "fish for people," but Jesus was using a reference that the people of that time could understand. Jesus also knew that the comparison would cause the disciples to get a mental picture of "catching people" and bringing them to God.

Special Materials Needed:
- small photograph of each child, or a cutout to represent each child (refer to paper dolls from the "A Prayer Table for Young Children" activity, page 11)
- a mesh bag (like the kind that holds oranges, potatoes, or onions) to represent a "net" with the words "I will make you fishers of people" attached on a label
- a poster board

Directions:
1. On a small piece of poster board trace and cut out the pattern of a fish. Cut angles on each fish to hold the photo. Insert the photo.

Additional Activities:
- Have the children sit in a circle. Discuss how we are all coming to Jesus and he is the "fisher of all people."
- Hold the mesh "net." Allow each child to come up and put his or her fish in the net. Sing to the tune of "Mulberry Bush:"

"We all come to Jesus, Jesus, Jesus.
    We all come to Jesus.
        Yes, we do."

"(Child's Name) comes to Jesus, Jesus, Jesus.
    We all come to Jesus.
        Yes, we do."

A Butterfly to Share

The butterfly has long been a symbol of Easter rebirth.

There are many crafts for making lovely butterflies. This one is different since it starts with a piece of candy. Let the candy lift your spirits in the same way that the sight of a graceful butterfly brightens your day.

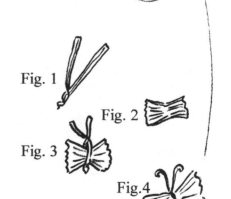

Special Materials Needed:
*   two wired paper baggy ties for each butterfly
*   individually wrapped candies in shiny papers

Directions:
1. Twist the two baggy ties together at one end (fig. 1).
2. Eat the candy! Smooth the wrapper.
3. Accordion-fold the wrapper in the center (fig. 2).
4. Place the accordion center between the two baggy ties.
5. Twist the baggy ties to hold the wrapper (fig. 3).
6. Curl the baggy tie top to make antennae.
7. Open the butterfly wings (fig. 4).

Additional Activities:
*   Have the children share the butterfly with a parent or friend.
*   Make a bulletin board with the butterflies.
*   Combine the butterfly with the Passion Vine on page 88.
*   Have the children make a flying, puppet butterfly by hanging the butterfly from the end of a straw or stick using thread.
*   Make a butterfly tree by hanging the butterflies from a dried limb that has been placed in a can or jar filled with pebbles or marbles.
*   Glue the butterfly to a special card or gift tag.

Mosaic Fun

Mosaics are fun for children. They love to see how small bits of paper will, especially when viewed from afar, produce a picture of relief and texture. Mosaics are an easy way to encourage working together—and a great way to use up small scraps of paper!

Children work together well when they can see a product being produced.

These projects allow all ability levels to work together on a project and achieve success. Here are some particular suggestions for mosaics. Directions for a separate craft follows.

- Make a bulletin board mosaic as a class project for a specific season. Provide an outline that the students fill with squares.
- Make an incentive bulletin board mosaic. When the children are well behaved, reward them with five squares to place on the mosaic.
- Combine the mosaic idea with a specific seasonal theme for making cards, posters, or banners.
- Mosaic something special such as a butterfly's wings, a cutout of an egg shape or a peace dove.

Special Materials Needed:
- colored paper scraps
- zipper-close baggies
- white or manila construction paper or poster board
- cotton-tipped swab or toothpick

Directions:
1. Cut or tear paper squares as desired. Store in zipper-close baggies by color.
2. Draw an outline of a religious image or print an inspirational phrase in block letters.
3. Use a toothpick or cotton-tipped swab dipped in glue to fill in the outline with colored pieces of paper.
4. Specify, or have the children designate specific colors for areas, if necessary.

Some ideas:

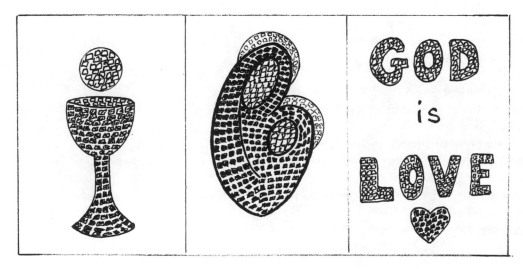

Endnotes

1 Prayer

Ich bin Klein, "Heritage Prayer", Traditional, author unknown.

"Prayer Table" reference from *Bundles of Faith and Tons of Fun* by Patricia Mathson (Notre Dame, IN: Ave Maria Press, 2000).

"Thank You 'Copters" adapted from spinner idea shared at St. Mary School, Ft. Walton Beach, FL.

2 Liturgy

For additional references to "Two Main Parts of the Mass" see: *Children Discover the Mass* by Mary Doerfler Dall (Notre Dame, IN: Ave Maria Press, 2000).

Straight Answers: The Color of Liturgical Vestments by Fr. William Saunders in "Arlington Catholic Herald," March 16, 1995 (courtesy of EWTN online).

3 The Bible

For additional references to "Jesus Loves the Little Children" see *Making Hallelujah Hats: Crafts and Activities Based on Bible Stories* by Mary Doerfler Dall (Mahwah, NJ: Paulist Press, 1998).

4 Legends and Lore

For additional references to "How the Ladybug Got Its Name" see
http://www.montana.edu/wwwpb/univ/bugnames.html

For additional references to "St. Patrick's Shamrock" see http://bhort.bh.cornell.edu/conservatory/cpage3.html

For additional references on poinsettias, candy canes, and holly see
http://www.hoover.nara.gov/gallery/legendx-mas-poinsettia.html
http://www.hoover.nara.gov/gallery/legendx-mas-candy.html
http://www.hoover.nara.gov/gallery/legendx-mas-holly.html

For additional references on Christmas trees see
http://botany.about.com/science/botany/library/weekly/aa122397.htm

For additional information on Christmas legends see:
http://www.geocities.com/Heartland/Acres/1170/candycane.html

For additional information on marigolds, lilies, eggs, and passion flowers see:
http://www.geocities.com/Heartland/Praries/5357/m.html
http://www.geocities.com/Heartland/Praries/5357m.html

http://www.geocities.com/Heartland/Praries/8149/egg.html
http://www.geocities.com/p-taggett/passionlgnd.html

Other references to holidays and liturgical seasons can be found at *Catholic Encyclopedia On-line* at www.newadvent.org/cathen/

5 Holy Days and Church Seasons

The "Miniature Advent Wreath" was adapted from an idea presented at St. Mary School, Ft. Walton Beach, FL.

General references found at *Catholic Encyclopedia On-Line*: www.newadvent.org/cathen/

6 More Faith Sharing

For more information on St. Francis see Catholic.org/saints. "Stone by Stone," excerpts from *The Sun and Moon Over Assisi: A Personal Encounter With Francis and Clare* by Gerard Thomas Straub.

Solution to Apostle Word Find p. 115

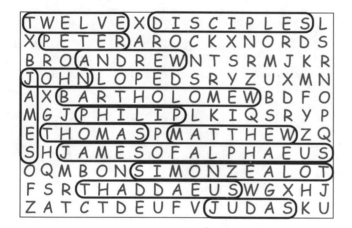